# BORDER WARS

# BORDER WARS

Tom Barry

DISCARD

A Boston Review Book

THE MIT PRESS Cambridge, Mass. London, England

MIT Press books may be purchased at special quantity discounts
for business or sales promotional use. For information, please
email special_sales@mitpress.mit.edu or write to Special Sales
Department, The MIT Press, 55 Hayward Street, Cambridge, MA
02142.

This book was set in Adobe Garamond by *Boston Review*
and was printed and bound in the United States of America.

Library of Congress Cataloging-in-Publication Data
Barry, Tom, 1950–
Border wars / Tom Barry.
    p.   cm. — (Boston Review books)
ISBN 978-0-262-01667-4 (hardcover : alk. paper)
1. United States—Emigration and immigration—Government
policy.  2. Mexican-American Border Region—Emigration and
immigration.  3. Border security—Government policy—United
States.  4. Border security—Economic aspects—Mexican-
American Border Region.  5. Immigration enforcement—Corrupt
practices—Mexican-American Border Region.  6. Political
corruption—Mexican-American Border Region.  7. Immigrants—
United States—Social conditions.  8. Mexican-American Border
Region—Social conditions.  I. Title.
JV6483.B375   2011
363.28'50973—dc23

                                                2011021039

10   9   8   7   6   5   4   3   2   1

*To Graciela and Jesus Galindo, loving parents of Jesus Manuel Galindo, who, on December 12, 2008, fell victim to the border wars in the immigrant prison in Pecos, Texas.*

# CONTENTS

*Introduction*

THE FLAG FLUTTERS AT HALF-MAST AT the Border Patrol checkpoint not far from the remote West Texas town of Sierra Blanca, in Hudspeth Country. Extending to the west, as far as you can see, are two lines of trucks and cars waiting for inspection.

To the south, a ribbon of dense riparian vegetation in the distance parallels the march of Interstate 10 from El Paso. On the other side lies Mexico and one of the deadliest places in the world—the killing fields of the Valle de Juárez in the border state of Chihuahua.

Both the highway checkpoint and the nearby town stand on the frontline of the nation's post-9/11 campaign for "border security." The county spreads

75 miles along the border, and signs of the border security buildup are everywhere: proliferating Border Patrol agents, the new steel fence that rises ominously along the river, sheriff's deputies enlisted for border duty.

Since 9/11, security budgets in the United States have become sacrosanct; the nation now spends $15 billion annually for border security. Despite the mounting federal budget deficit, Democrats and Republicans compete with each other to burnish their border security credentials with new spending proposals.

But basic questions have gone largely unaddressed.

If the buildup in border security infrastructure is indeed improving security, then this should be evident in places such as Hudspeth County. In the past ten years, the county sheriff's department has received millions of dollars in federal grants for border patrols. The number of Border Patrol agents stationed there has more than tripled. The checkpoint, now open day and night, counts on a full deployment of K-9 teams to aid inspections. And, of course, there's the fence.

While there is certainly more control, more security operations in this swath of borderland, there is good reason to doubt that we are getting our money's worth. Close up in Hudspeth County, border security policy seems, at best, misdirected, at worst, pure folly characterized by escalating marijuana-user arrests, inter-agency tensions, opportunistic threat analysis, enormous waste, and ideological posturing. No terrorists have been apprehended.

The sheriff's caseload has increased five-fold, and the poor county now depends on the revenue generated by the $750 fines regularly meted out to motorists caught on the interstate highway with a marijuana pipe or personal stash. "They come here driving from California, fat and happy, passing through with their pot," Deputy Sheriff Mike Doyle explained while showing me the department's overflowing evidence room. "But Texas has its own laws, and we take drug violations seriously."

What is true in Hudspeth County holds across the length of the nearly 2,000–mile southwestern border. Apprehensions of illegal immigrants are down dramatically, but seizures of drugs, particularly marijuana, stand at record highs.

Especially in Texas and Arizona, local officials could not be happier about these arrangements. Politicians and law enforcement rake in federal dollars for dubious security projects. In both states, those same officials tout the projects as their own valiant efforts to do what the federal government won't, and they go further, offering their methods as national models.

Yet there's no disputing that the border has become a more dangerous place—not just in the killing fields on the other side but also on the U.S. side. It's just that the dangers, having nothing to do with terrorism, are largely of our own manufacture.

While U.S. communities experience little spillover violence directly related to the Mexican drug war and drug trafficking—El Paso is the safest large city in the nation—illegal border crossings are increasingly associated with armed criminal enterprises. That's why the flag fluttered at half-mast. As a Border Patrol agent who escorted me around the checkpoint explained, a member of the Patrol's BORTAC unit (a SWAT team) had just been killed on the border by a gang of Mexican bandits who, armed with semi-automatic weapons purchased legally in Arizona, had been preying on smugglers and illegal immigrants. As the border has grown more fortified on the U.S. side, illegal crossing has become costlier and more challenging. It is no longer possible to cross the border illegally without paying human smugglers to navigate the difficult course.

Similarly the difficulty and costs of crossing drugs have increased, and, as the fight among smuggling organizations to control the drug-trafficking *plazas* has intensified, cross-border drug smugglers have armed themselves. The Mexican drug war and the U.S. border security crackdown have given rise to a new wave of criminality at the border in the form of highly armed bandits who seize drug loads and rob immigrants and their guides.

In other words, thanks in part to U.S. government attempts to secure the border—itself an outgrowth of the failures to pass comprehensive and just immigration reform and to handle drug policy effectively—the border has grown more violent. In Mexico, the drug war declared by the President Felipe Calderón in December 2006—since waged with U.S. logistical and financial support—has given rise to a level of violence not experienced since the era of the Mexican Revolution. Both along the border and in Mexico itself, security appears an increasingly unattainable goal.

I TRAVELED ALONG THE SOUTHWESTERN BORder, focusing on Texas and Arizona, seeking out the local and national impact and politics of these security campaigns.

I start in Pecos, Texas, with the death from gross medical neglect of an immigrant detainee, Jesus

Galindo, at a privately operated, government-owned prison. His wrongful death on December 12, 2008 enraged fellow inmates, ignited two riots, and sparked the ACLU of Texas to file a major lawsuit that lays bare the utter lack of the rule of law in immigrant detention.

Sheriff Arvin West of Hudspeth County is the county official in charge of the Sierra Blanca prison that once held Galindo. As chairman of the Texas Border Sheriffs Coalition, Sheriff West figures prominently in what Governor Rick Perry calls the "Texas border security model," the subject of the book's second chapter.

With its 1,200 miles of border, Texas is a major player in the border security bandwagon. Alarmist cries by border politicians about spillover violence and insufficient federal attention to the border have successfully pressured the federal government to direct large flows of funding to state and local law enforcement agencies, creating not only a gravy train of federal grants but also a platform for right-wing populism. As played out so extravagantly in Texas, border security and homeland security have become prey for political opportunism, ideological fantasizing, and grant-grabbing.

Arizona has launched its own vision of border security and immigration enforcement, a vision that has proved influential among other state and local governments. This is the subject of the book's third essay. Tapping the popular fears and resentment associated with immigration and the border, right-wing politicians and sheriffs, such as Governor Jan Brewer and Sheriffs Paul Babeu and Larry Dever, have consolidated their political bases in Arizona and gained a national hearing for hard-line, albeit simplistic, programs. Their Washington-bashing is wildly popular, but rarely do they acknowledge just how dependent on federal funding are state government and border law enforcement. The often-bizarre politics of border security and immigration in Arizona point to the urgent need for the federal government to reframe and reform its immigration, drug, criminal justice, and border policies.

Throughout my investigations I found that the border security push has injected new life into the war on drugs by reconfiguring those failed policies as vital components of national security. Immigration control, too, has been swallowed by the security paradigm. Instead of reforming the economic incentives that make illegal immigration inevitable, the United States has been stuffing non-threatening people into for-profit prisons. Counterterrorism, the ostensible purpose of these undertakings, is an excuse for sheriffs to absorb federal subsidy. And the lack of a coherent border policy provides a vacuum in which reactionary populism and nationalism have flourished at the local, state, and federal levels.

Policy and operations should target core problems. That's never been the case with U.S. border control, and this disjuncture between policy and problem-solving has widened over the past decade. Since border control has been framed as a security issue, there has been less political space to question the value and cost of border control operations. As the national security bandwagon rolls on, the cost—in dollars and human lives—is very high indeed.

# 1

*A Death in Texas*

County Clerk Dianne Florez noticed it first. Plumes of smoke were rising outside the small West Texas town of Pecos. "The prison is burning again," she announced.

About a month and a half before, on December 12, 2008, inmates had rioted to protest the death of one of their own, Jesus Manuel Galindo. When the 32-year-old Galindo's body was removed from the prison in what looked to them like a large black trash bag, they set fire to the recreational center and occupied the exercise yard overnight. Using smuggled cell phones, they told worried family members and the media about poor medical care in the prison and described the treatment of Galindo, who had been in solitary confinement since mid-November. During that time, fellow inmates and his mother, who called the prison nearly every day, had warned authorities that Galindo needed daily medication for epilepsy and was suffering from severe seizures in the "security housing unit," which the inmates call the "hole."

I arrived in Pecos on February 2, 2009 shortly after the second riot broke out. I had driven 200 miles east from El Paso through the northern reaches of the Chihuahuan desert.

Pecos is the seat of Reeves County in "far West" Texas and home to what the prison giant GEO Group calls "the largest detention/correctional facility under private management in the world." The prison, a sprawling complex surrounded by forbidding perimeter fences on the town's deserted southwestern edge, holds up to 3,700 inmates. Almost all are serving time in federal lockup before being deported and are what the Departments of Justice and Homeland Security (DHS) call "criminal aliens."

Although the term "criminal aliens" has no precise definition, its broadening use reflects a trend in dealing with immigrants. With the post-9/11 creation of DHS and its two agencies—Immigration and Customs Enforcement (ICE) and Customs and Border Protection (CBP)—a wide sector of aliens increasingly became the focus of joint efforts by immigration and law enforcement officers. ICE's Criminal Alien Program, working with local police, began targeting for deportation both legal and illegal immigrants with criminal records. And CBP's Border Patrol began to turn over illegal border crossers to the justice system for criminal prosecution, instead of, as in the past, simply deporting them. Many criminal aliens are long-term legal residents of the United States and are also the parents, children, or siblings of U.S. citizens and other lawful residents.

When the prison started burning again, I was in the county clerk's office tracking down the agreements, contracts, and subcontracts that establish the paper foundation of the Reeves County Detention

Complex, the oldest county-owned immigrant prison, constructed as a speculative venture and opened in 1988. Since 2001, immigration prisons such as Reeves have boomed along the border in Texas, New Mexico, and Arizona. Some hold ICE detainees, some U.S. Marshals Service (USMS) detainees, and others, like the one in Reeves, prisoners of the Federal Bureau of Prisons (BOP). Despite this alphabet soup, in the nine months I traveled along the southwestern border visiting eleven prison towns, all the prisons I saw had two common features: they were managed and operated by private-prison corporations—including two of the world's largest, Corrections Corporation of America (CCA) and GEO—and they were located in remote, rural areas, invariably described by locals as being "in the middle of nowhere."

These immigration prisons constitute the new face of imprisonment in America: the speculative public-private prison, publicly owned by local governments, privately operated by corporations, publicly financed by tax-exempt bonds, and located in depressed communities. Because they rely on project revenue instead of tax revenue, these prisons do not need voter approval. Instead they are marketed by prison consultants to municipal and county governments as economic-development tools promising job creation and new revenue without new taxes. The possibility of riots usually goes unmentioned.

Sirens blared outside the Complex as an array of law enforcement forces—county deputies, city police, Border Patrol agents, state police, and GEO's own security guards—rushed toward it. Inmates had set fire to a housing unit this time. David Galindo, Jesus's brother, told a reporter, "They're afraid somebody might die there again." According to one inmate, jailors placed a detainee, 25-year-old Ramon Garcia, in solitary confinement after he complained of dizziness and feeling ill. "All we wanted was for them to give him medical care and because they didn't, things got out of control and people started fires in several offices," said the inmate, who declined to give his name for fear of reprisals by officials.

As smoke billowed up from the prison on that early February morning, officials and staff at the county building expressed more resentment than concern. Florez complained that the inmates can count on three meals a day and a television to watch while they idle their time away. Not to mention that their rent and electricity bills get paid, while Pecos residents have to work every day to make ends meet. (In September 2009 the unemployment rate in Reeves County—whose 13,300 residents have a per capita income of $10,800 a year—topped 14 percent.) Others worried for the jobs of more than 400 county residents who worked at the prison and about the cost of repairing the damaged buildings.

"You can be sure that we will be paying for it," lamented one county employee.

## Becoming a Prison Town

The Pecos of the mythical Pecos Bill and the "Home of the World's First Rodeo" was a famous cowboy crossroads where the Pecos River met the Butterfield

Route, Chisholm Trail, and Loving-Goodnight Trail. In the late 1800s, rowdy saloons began giving way to more wholesome establishments and hotels, and Pecos became a major transportation hub with the arrival of the Texas and Pacific Railroad. For almost a century, a progression of railway men, cotton farmers, ranchers, oil riggers, wildcatters, and B-1 pilots filled the streets.

But the oil riggers and wildcatters began leaving town in the early 1980s. Except for the county courthouse, the sheriff's office, and a few remaining retail stores, downtown Pecos is now dead. The old railway depots are shut down; the Santa Fe depot was sold off for its aged bricks and timber to a steakhouse in Odessa, an hour down the interstate. With the railroad companies long since gone, and ranching, cotton, and oil booms collapsing, Pecos is valued today not as a transportation and distribution center but rather for its isolation and economic desperation.

Debbie Thomas, curator of the West of the Pecos Museum (commonly known as the cowboy museum), sighs when asked about the town's only steady business over the past two decades. "Well, we don't want to be known as a prison town, but it's better than being a ghost town," she says.

In 1985 Reeves County became the first of a few dozen Texas counties to get into the speculative prison business, when Judge Jimmy Galindo (no relation to Jesus Manuel Galindo) persuaded the County Commissioners Court to take a bold step for Pecos's economic future. At the time, Judge Galindo and other county leaders argued that Pecos could cash in on the surge in incarceration rates that accompanied the war on drugs. Years later, for the prison's two expansions, the county and the private operators would rely on the federal government to send them immigrant inmates.

Indeed, immigrant detention has been central to the growth of the "privates" for more than two decades. The Immigration and Naturalization Service's (INS) 1983 decision to outsource immigrant detention to the newly established Corrections Corporation of America gave birth to the private-prison industry; GEO Group (formerly Wackenhut) got its start imprisoning immigrants in the late 1980s.

While the nation's nonimmigrant prison population has recently leveled off, the number of immigrants in ICE (formerly INS) detention has increased fivefold since the mid-1990s, and continues year after year to reach record highs. In 2010 ICE detained a record number of immigrants—more than 392,000. ICE projects that as many as 440,000 immigrants will be deported in 2011.

The federal government's escalating demand for immigrant prison beds saved CCA and other privates that had overbuilt speculative prisons. Since 2001 the prison giants CCA ($1.7 billion in annual revenue) and GEO Group ($1.2 billion) have racked up record profits, with jumps in revenue and profits roughly paralleling the rising numbers of detained immigrants.

Initially, most speculative prisons were privately owned, a case of the federal government outsourcing its responsibilities. But prison outsourcing is rarely that simple anymore. The private-prison industry increasingly works with local governments to establish and operate speculative prisons. Prison-town officials have a mantra: "If you build a prison the prisoners will come."

Most of the time, these public-private prisons are only speculative ventures for bondholders and local governments because agreements signed with federal agencies do not guarantee prisoners. For the privates, however, risks are low and the rewards large. Usually paid a set fee by local governments to operate prisons, management companies have no capital investment and lose little, other than hefty monthly fees, if inmate flows from the federal government decline or stop.

Prisons are owned by local governments, but local oversight of finances is rare, and the conditions of prisoners are often ignored. Inmates such as those in Pecos are technically in the custody of the federal government, but they are in fact in the custody of corporations with little or no federal supervision. So labyrinthine are the contracting and financing arrangements that there are no clear pathways to determine responsibility and accountability. Yet every contract provides an obvious and unimpeded flow of money to the private industry and consultants.

In the case of immigration prisons, BOP, USMS, and ICE sign intergovernmental agreements and contracts with local governments, generally in remote, economically deprived communities. A prison consultancy such as Innovative Government Strategies (IGS), a Texas-based firm that specializes in selling private-prison projects to rural governments, coordinates the deal.

Most often, a team of private-prison intermediaries—bond brokers, design and construction firms, law firms—are brought together by the consultancy, which is fronting for a prison-management company. The consultant and these private clients plant the idea of prison-led development with one or two key community officials, and then wine, dine, and fly them around to other prisons to sell and seal the deal. The lead official promotes the project in the community as his or her brainchild.

Once other county commissioners are also persuaded by the grand promises of prison-led development, the county commission sets up a paper "public facility corporation" for the sole purpose of issuing so-called project revenue bonds—secured not by the general revenues of the issuing government but by those from the bond-financed project—to fund the prison. This corporation then leases the project back to the county government, which signs an agreement with a federal agency that authorizes it to hold federal prisoners. The county, in turn, subcontracts the responsibility for managing and operating to the private-prison firm represented by the consultant. In many cases the rural government also subcontracts responsibility for medical services to a provider specializing in "correctional health services."

Project revenues are the per diems paid by the feds—BOP, USMS, or ICE—or by the corrections departments of the state governments. In the case of

ICE, these per diems now average $87 for every "man day." But since the bondholders own the prison, the payments go not to the county but to a trustee established to manage the payments to the bondholders and all other parties in the prison project—county, consultants, builders, and prison operator.

County governments see a new revenue stream from the federal per diem—usually a mere $1–2 a day per inmate, depending on the terms of the agreement with the prison operator—but only after the bondholders and private operator have been paid. The privates receive hefty operating fees (normally $500,000–$750,000 a month) and salaries for their administrative team of wardens and assistants, while assuming none of the capital, operating, or maintenance costs. Because the prisons are public facilities, communities receive no property or sales tax revenue (from construction and maintenance) but are expected to provide water and sewage services.

In Hudspeth County, Judge Becky Dean-Walker signs the agreements and contracts that have, since

2003, made Sierra Blanca an immigrant-prison town. Situated 90 miles from El Paso, Sierra Blanca—population 533, according to the 2000 U.S. Census—hosts the West Texas Detention Facility, a 500-bed immigrant prison with another 500 still-unoccupied beds in three adjoining structures awaiting overflow. The prison, a public-private complex, is owned by bondholders until 2025.

In establishing the prison on the edge of town, Hudspeth, where one in three families survives under the poverty line, incurred a $23.5 million debt in revenue bonds, plus $15.5 million in interest. Seven years after the immigrant prison opened, the county faced $36.1 million in outstanding debt servicing. According to the Texas Bond Review Board, the $20.5 million in remaining principal on the prison bonds translates into a per capita debt ratio of $6,611—debt divided by population—for residents of Hudspeth County, one of the poorest in the nation.

Emerald Corrections, a Shreveport, Louisiana-based corrections-management company, and its intermediaries promoted the prison as an economic-development project, promising jobs and income growth. But only a few locals work at the facility, with most employees bused every morning from El Paso.

When the bonds mature in 2025, the facility will be a badly depreciated investment, a community eyesore, and a reminder of the delusional dreams of prison-based economic development. This is true in many parts of Texas, such as Encinal, a town even poorer than Sierra Blanca, with its very own Emerald-operated prison thanks to an identical arrangement of consultancies, bond brokers, contractors, and county officials. IGS walked away with a reported $700,000 in consultancy fees.

Bill Addington, who lives within easy sight of the prison in Sierra Blanca and who opposed the prison proposal, said the prison was approved by the county without any involvement in or specific knowledge of the bond agreement or operating agreements. In fact, no one in county government could find the agreement with USMS or the bond-issuing statement, or even remember their details.

Hudspeth is hardly alone in this regard. Local governments typically do not have anyone to keep track of the complex prison business—a high-finance enterprise involving tens of millions of dollars in bonds (more than $130 million in Reeves County) and millions of dollars in annual federal payments. Not only had contracts seemingly disappeared in the counties I visited, county employees could not locate full accountings of prison-related expenses and income.

At a public meeting to consider the proposal for the first immigrant prison in Otero County, New Mexico, county resident George Bussing captured the confusion. "I'm smarter than most average bears," he said, "but I honestly don't understand what I'm reading here."

Despite dubious benefits to local economies, new prisons continue to spring up. District chairman Austin Nuñez of the Tohono O'odham Nation has been trying to use tax-exempt project revenue bonds to finance a prison for immigrants on tribal land south of Tucson, in the district of San Xavier. He has described the proposed prison as an "economic-development project" that will bring jobs and revenue to this poor Native American community that spans the U.S.-Mexico border.

IGS is making the necessary arrangements. All the San Xavier District has to do is sign a contract agreeing to subcontract its imprisonment authority to a private-prison company.

The same team of private-prison intermediaries that interested the Tohono O'odham community in prison-based economic development also enticed a poor community in Montana. Four years after construction—with the bond fund depleted from payouts to the prison consultants, design and construction firms, and bond underwriters—the prison in Hardin, Montana stands empty, and the local development authority that issued the bonds has defaulted. At one point, the authority tried with the Obama administration to hold Guantánamo Bay detainees there.

"I believe the people of Hardin were duped by these construction people out of Texas to build the facility, then the bond people to build this," Montana governor Brian Schweitzer said.

There is no paper trail that explains how these speculative prisons secure federal contracts. But like most scenarios in which public governance meets private business, the partnerships are usually the product of connections and influence, highly paid friends in the right places.

That was the case in 2004 when Judge Galindo overrode the objections of a Reeves County auditor in his bid to hire Public-Private Strategies Consulting to represent the interests of the Reeves County Detention Center to the BOP. The firm's president, Randy DeLay, charged $120,000 a year plus expenses, but hiring him may have made good political sense. Randy's famous last name is no coincidence—his brother Tom, the Texas Republican, was the House majority leader at the time. Reeves County secured one of four BOP prison contracts for detaining criminal aliens the following year. Judge Galindo was unequivocal about Randy DeLay's usefulness, arguing that he was able to get meetings with people in Washington, D.C.: "I think it's vital that we have a direct line into the inner workings," Galindo told the Commissioners Court.

## Immigration on Trial

Though speculative prisons come with no guarantees, all along the southwestern border—from Florence, Arizona to Raymondville, Texas—business is good. Since early 2003, the criminal justice and immigration enforcement systems have merged, breaking the longstanding tradition of treating immigration violations as administrative offenses and creating hundreds of thousands of new criminal aliens.

While the growth in immigrant detention is in part due to the country's increased immigrant population, the shift in immigration policy away from regulation and toward enforcement, punishment, and deterrence is more significant. Unwilling to pass a reform bill that would effectively regulate immigration, Congress and the executive branch have turned to the criminal justice and penal systems.

New anti-immigrant laws and practices by ICE and CBP subject immigrants, legal or illegal, to double jeopardy, punishing them twice for the same offense. In 1996 the Republican majority in Congress led approval of three anti-immigrant and anti-crime laws that spurred INS to start cracking down on and deporting immigrants. These laws, together with the executive branch's increased authority to devise repressive immigration procedures under the post-9/11 pretext of the war on terrorism, have created an enforcement regime in which noncitizen legal immigrants face immigration consequences (as well as criminal consequences) for past or present violations of criminal law. In other words, illegal immigrants and even noncitizen permanent residents may be jailed *and* deported for committing crimes or other offenses, whether violent or not. DHS and the Justice Department are not only combing the criminal justice system for legal and illegal immigrants to be detained and deported, but the departments are also working together to transfer illegal immigrants into federal courts and prisons. Legal scholars have taken to calling this merger of criminal and immigration law and the integration of the criminal justice and immigration systems "crimmigration."

Private-prison executives are particularly upbeat about new criminal-alien programs such as CBP's Operation Streamline and ICE's Secure Communities. GEO Chairman George Zoley told Wall Street analysts in a July 2009 investment conference call, "The main driver for the growth of new beds at the federal level continues to be the detention and incarceration of criminal aliens." CCA's Chief Financial Officer, Todd Mullenger, emphasized the importance of programs such as Operation Streamline to prison profits in a recent investment conference call:

> Border Patrol has consistently indicated from the planning stage of the initiative to the present that Operation Streamline will require additional detain beds due

to increased prosecution and length of stay anticipated by the initiative.

Operation Streamline was launched in 2005 as a pilot project of the Del Rio sector of Texas and extends east to the southern Rio Grande Valley and west to Yuma, Arizona. It is part of a national immigrant crackdown that CBP and ICE variously call "enhanced enforcement" and "zero tolerance." The program directs Border Patrol agents to turn captured illegal border crossers over to the Marshals for prosecution, breaking with the usual practice of simply returning Mexican immigrants to Mexico or releasing non-Mexican immigrants with an order to appear in immigration court.

A few mornings each week, detainees pack the federal courtroom in Del Rio, Texas, where they plead guilty to illegal entry and are sentenced as criminals. The scene in Judge Dennis Green's chamber is replicated along much of the border. While the courtroom is quickly filling, Del Rio's nearby Main

Street, which once bustled with shoppers from Ciudad Acuña across the river, is quiet, lined with empty and closed stores.

More than four-dozen young men and eight young women shuffle into the courtroom on April 17, 2009, occupying the seats normally reserved for visitors and family members. Only at the last minute do the security guards allow me in, after determining that the back row will not be occupied by the day's crowd of criminal aliens.

The clinking of chains fills the room as the accused are ushered into their seats. Handcuffed, chained from waist to ankles, they stand then sit in unison when ordered by the attending U.S. marshals.

The scene was shocking the first time, but now I have witnessed it in three courts of justice in the borderlands: shackled immigrants filling up the courtrooms, and then, after an hour or two, shuffling out, where they are taken back to USMS detention centers or a BOP prison. At first I wondered if their laceless running shoes and work boots, with their tongues hanging loose, were a new style for young Mexicans. But later I understood that the marshals obligated them to surrender the laces (as possible weapons or suicide instruments) and that this, not the chains, explains why they walk without lifting their feet out of their shoes.

At these mass convictions and sentencings, I was in a small minority. The judges, the marshals, the lawyers, the security guards, and me—all white and older, with jobs and homes. And them: criminal aliens, all young and lean, most with strong arms and calloused hands, all with black hair and weathered brown skin. These courtrooms are where the South encounters the North, where the exclusionary institutions on one side of the global economic divide collide with collective desperation on the other. The power imbalance, so starkly visible, is startling.

Before starting the overland journey north— sometimes from as far as Honduras, El Salvador, and Guatemala—each immigrant understood that he or she was an economic castoff, marginalized by national and global economic forces. But each hoped that the United States would be what so many claim: the land of opportunity, where class and circumstances are no barrier to economic security, as long as you are willing to work hard.

Judge Green enters. "All rise," intones the court sergeant at arms, and the immigrants stand up, following the Spanish echo of their bilingual courtroom manager.

Over the past day or two, each prisoner has told his or her story in a few minutes to a paralegal who has organized a two-sentence defense.

Unlike the U.S. criminal justice system, immigration law provides no guarantees that all accused have the right to a court-appointed lawyer. Those facing criminal charges in federal court for immigration violations, however, do get free legal defense, but it is pro forma—a windfall for many regional attorneys who thrive on government fees for nominal defense work. On April 17 Judge Green publicly applauded the immigrants' attorney, who had recently been appointed to take his place on the bench. The congratulatory comment went untranslated.

One by one, the defendants are escorted to the front of the court. A CBP lawyer tells the judge that the accused has crossed the border between the ports of entry without inspection (violating U.S. Code Title 8, 1325) and recounts any previous record of illegal entry or criminal conviction.

More than 50 individual criminal hearings are streamlined—a possible explanation of the operation's name—with the same judge, same defender, and same outcome: guilty as charged and remanded for incarceration.

Before each case is heard and before each defendant is sentenced, Judge Green asks them en masse if they have had time to consult their attorney, if they have been forced or threatened to plead guilty, if they have knowingly violated the laws of the United States of America by crossing without inspection. They reply in a chorus of "*Sí*" and "*No*," bringing to mind an elementary school classroom.

Could one gather a group of unfamiliar U.S. citizens and see such cooperation, such compliance?

As each faces the judge, their collective defense attorney reads from a sheet his assistant has prepared with the abbreviated stories and pleas for mercy from this mass of immigrants.

No one has more than an eighth-grade education, three out of four cite medical emergencies, all crossed to seek work and food, and many hoped to reunite with families that need them. Story after abbreviated story of fathers, mothers, wives, and children with brain tumors, heart conditions, crippling accidents, no work, and little to eat.

Judge Green occasionally expresses sympathy, encourages them to secure a visa the next time they want to come to the United States—a near impossibility for Latin Americans with no bank accounts and no property and utterly out of the question for these detainees, imprisoned and eventually deported for illegal entry—and then asks if they are guilty of breaking the laws of this country by entering without permission. One after another they say, "culpable" or "guilty."

Before sentencing, the judge warns those who have never been previously deported that they will be judged felons if they are caught in the future. Depending on the time they have already spent in jail, they are sentenced up to twelve days. Those with a record of previous illegal crossings get harsher sentences, routinely as much as 180 days and sometimes several years. Although the charge is always illegal entry or reentry, the sentence varies based on the number of illegal entries, whether the charged immigrant has a criminal record, and the judge's discretion.

The defense attorney and government prosecutors pack up their papers and leave the courtroom. Any hope on the part of an immigrant that the judge would find mercy is now dashed. Ordered to stand, the convicted and sentenced immigrants rise together, and, row by row, exit the courtroom, feet dragging in their laceless shoes. It's back to the GEO prison whence they came that morning.

Between apprehension and removal, an unauthorized immigrant who is criminally prosecuted is technically in the custody of, first, CBP or ICE, then the Marshals Service, and finally BOP or the Marshals Service again. Depending on how long it takes ICE to prepare the removal papers and to present its case before the immigration court, immigrants may spend anywhere from a week to several years in detention before being deported.

With its staggering administrative, legal, and detention costs, Operation Streamline is certainly not quick and easy. But the initiative is less about law than strategy. The idea is that, having suffered the humiliation of being branded a criminal and spending time in prison, these immigrants will not come back once deported and will tell others that the price of immigration is too high. As DHS Secretary Michael Chertoff explained in 2006, "We are working to get [Operation Streamline] expanded across other parts of the border" because "it has a great deterrent effect."

Measured by the number of immigrants apprehended in the Del Rio sector and others, immigration flows have decreased markedly, although no one can say to what extent the drop is a result of deterrence as opposed to the recession. But five years after the program's initiation, immigrants keep crossing the river at Del Rio and elsewhere along the border where the program is in effect. What strategy of deterrence could stop those forced to leave their families from attempting, even at the risk of increased jail time, to return to their loved ones back home in the United States?

## *Mala Suerte*

Jesus Manuel Galindo, a native of Ciudad Juárez, had compelling reasons to come to the United States. He was twice married to legal U.S. residents, and his children are American citizens. His parents, originally from the Mexican state of Chihuahua, are both legal U.S. residents. They live in the border *colonia* of Anthony, New Mexico, just outside El Paso. They obtained legal residency for their younger son and daughter and were in the process of getting papers for Jesus, their oldest. They told me it was easier to get papers for younger children.

In 2006 Jesus was picked up by the police when he had a seizure at a convenience store. When deputies checked his records and saw that he had no legal status, they turned him over to immigration officials. He was deported to Juárez, where he remained a month or so, determined to come back to his second wife and children.

According to his mother, Graciela, he had the "*mala suerte*," bad luck, to be caught by the Border Patrol. In the past the Border Patrol had just sent him back to Juárez. This time, he went first to the Otero County Prison Facility, and then spent three months in Sierra Blanca before being sent to Reeves County Detention Complex. Although he was convicted only of illegal entry, Galindo was sentenced to 30 months under a system of "penalty enhancement" that allows judges to add time for past crimes—in

Galindo's case, writing a hot check and contacting his ex-wife in violation of a restraining order—even if prior sentences were served. Galindo had already spent time in other Texas prisons for the check.

Graciela said he had been working hard at Sierra Blanca in the laundry trying to reduce his time for good behavior, but it did not count for anything. He did the same thing at Reeves until prison administrators told him he could no longer work because of his seizures.

On December 11 he wrote to his mother:

> Don't despair. . . . But tell the investigator [sent by federal public defenders] that I get sick here by being locked up all by myself. They don't even know and I am all bruised up [from falling and thrashing during seizures]. . . . Tell the investigator that the medical care in here is no good and that I'm scared. Well, mom, I love you very much. I will write you on Monday. Kisses to everyone.

On the morning of December 12, Graciela called the prison to see how he was. "They didn't want to talk to me. But I kept calling and then they told me that my son was dead."

Two years later th ACLU of Texas and El Paso attorneys Miguel Torres and Leon Schydlower filed a wrongful death complaint in El Paso federal court on behalf of Galindo's wife, three children, and parents. Torres calls Galindo's death a "quintessentially avoidable tragedy." The complaint—filed against GEO, Reeves County, the Federal Bureau of Prisons, and Physicians Network Association (PNA), the subcontractor responsible for medical care in the prison—describes how Galindo's death came after he, his family, and others attempted repeatedly to persuade prison and medical staff to move him out of isolation and provide effective medication to control his seizures.

According to Torres both Galindo's wife and his fellow inmates repeatedly urged prison officials to give him his medication and to get him out of the security housing unit (SHU)—solitary confinement—where he had been placed for medical observation in November after an emergency stay at an area hospital due to a severe seizure. Graciela mailed the prison her son's medical records, but they sent them back, instructing her not to send them again.

"U.S. taxpayer dollars were used to pay a for-profit medical provider with a documented record of providing constitutionally inadequate care, and federal officials looked the other way while inmates like Mr. Galindo were denied access to the most basic medical necessities," Lisa Graybill, Legal Director for the ACLU of Texas, said in a press release accompanying the lawsuit. "A prisoner's citizenship status does not matter when it comes to medical care—federal inmates are entitled to equal protection of the law, and no inmate held in a United States prison should be subject to the deliberate denial of life-saving medication, then left in solitary to die."

Galindo's father broke down as he discussed the conditions in which his son was kept:

We don't understand how there can be so little humanity there in the prison. Animals aren't even treated as badly as they treated our son, keeping him locked up in the hole so sick and without any company. It was so cruel, and he died sick and afraid.

In fact, lockdown in the SHU was Reeves's policy for all ailing inmates. At the time, the prison did not have an infirmary. After the riots, BOP requested that one be built as part of the prison reconstruction and upgrade. At a public discussion, then-County Judge Sam Contreras explained why the $1.8 million outlay was needed: "[The lack of infirmary beds is] what caused the disturbance—because [prisoners] were placed in the SHU when they didn't do nothing wrong. They are just sick."

Galindo is not the only casualty of a toxic mix of crackdown policies and a burgeoning public-private-prison complex. As of March 2011, 120 immigrants have died while in ICE custody. Given the lack of oversight and legal protections, the gains to be made from cost-cutting, and the apathy surrounding prisoner well-being, these deaths are predictable. Indeed, the county awarded the medical care subcontract to PNA primarily because the company boasted that it would reduce the county's expenses by cutting back on prescriptions, medical tests, and outside medical visits. And in this regard, according to former Reeves warden Rudy Franco, PNA did not fail.

### "They Want to Be on *American Idol*"

PNA is the brainchild of a Lubbock, Texas physician, Vernon Farthing. In 1991, after working as a contract doctor for Lubbock's county jail, Farthing started PNA, which he calls "a leader in correctional healthcare."

From his base in Lubbock, Farthing oversees operations in dozens of prisons in Texas, Arizona, and New Mexico. PNA and prison operator Management and Training Corporation (MTC) were the subjects of a federal civil rights investigation into conditions at Santa Fe County Detention Center, which houses a large population of Native American inmates. The investigation was sparked by the suicide of pretrial inmate Tyson Johnson, who suffered from severe claustrophobia and other mental illnesses.

In its report the Justice Department specified 52 actions needed "to rectify the identified deficiencies and to protect the constitutional rights of the facility's inmates to bring the jail into compliance with civil rights standards." Thirty-eight of the 52 identified deficiencies related to medical services. According to the report:

The Detention Center, through PNA, provides inadequate medical services in the following areas: intake, screening, and referral; acute care; emergent care; chronic and prenatal care; and medication administration and management. As a result, inmates at the Detention Center with serious medical needs are at risk for harm.

In a story on the investigation, Suzan Garcia, Johnson's mother, explained that she had tried to contact the jail because she was concerned about her son's psychological condition. "I called the jail and asked to speak to a doctor, but they said they didn't have a doctor," Garcia said. "When I asked to speak to the warden, they just put me on hold and then the phone would disconnect."

According to the Justice Department's findings and associated reports, Johnson had asked to see a psychologist, but the 580-inmate jail did not have one. Johnson was placed in solitary confinement, and managed to hang himself from a sprinkler head in his windowless cell.

Soon after the Justice Department released the results of its investigation, PNA pulled out of its sub-contract with MTC, claiming it could not continue because it was losing money. Within a year, MTC terminated its contract with the county, also claiming it was losing money.

Three years later, when seeking to renew its Reeves County contract, PNA submitted what was at best a misleading statement about its history of providing correctional health care. PNA told the county commission that it was "proud of its record of no substantiated grievances in any facility" and that it had "never had a contract canceled or been removed from a facility."

The riots at Reeves brought PNA's medical services to the attention of the Austin-based advocacy group Grassroots Leadership as well as the American Civil Liberties Union of Texas, both of which are now focusing on reform efforts. When asked about the liability that Reeves County may face if the inmates take their cases to court, County Attorney Alma Alvarez said she was not worried, noting that GEO and PNA had recently secured accreditation for the prison from both the American Correctional Association (ACA) and the Joint Commission on Accreditation of Healthcare Organizations. After visiting the prison herself, she said she was confident that the medical care was up to or above standards. She acknowledged, however, that she never spoke to any of the inmates about the quality of medical care, only to the administration.

Concerning the prisoner complaints made during the riots, Alvarez said, "They want to be media stars. They call the media from their cell phones and tell these stories because they want to be famous. It's like they want to be on *American Idol*."

A framed certificate of achievement from the ACA hangs on the wall of the prison's lobby. Awarded exactly a month after the December 12 riot, it honors the prison for "the attainment of excellence in adult correctional care."

Sheriff Andy Gomez said of Galindo's death, "We investigate all the deaths in the prison, but I can't remember every one." And Gomez summed up a common sentiment in Reeves County when it comes to prisoners' grievances about denial of medical attention: "These guys are criminals," he said. "They need to realize that they are in jail."

## Money for Nothing

Soon after opening its first immigrant prison, MTC named Otero County Administrator Ruth Hooser a "Community Supporter of the Year," describing her as "The Best of the Best" and placing her among the most appreciated public officials involved in eleven MTC correctional operations in the United States, Australia, and Canada. In accepting the award, Hooser said, "I just kept pushing and helping with whatever they needed."

County officials play the role of smart economic developers and prison companies respond with accolades and awards. The mutual admiration is on display in the waiting rooms of the prisons, where plaques from local chambers of commerce praising companies' civic virtues, statements of appreciation from the high school marching band or football team, and award certificates from the prison operators plaster the walls. At least in prison towns along the border, there is nearly universal agreement that the prison business is like any other.

Yet, while most government officials passively accept the conditions of the prison deals, and hardly anyone harbors moral reservations about the business, in some towns, including Pecos, locals grumble that they should be getting a greater share of the revenue.

In Reeves County, many believe that the county could do a better job of running the prison than GEO.

"We pay the same management fees and salaries to GEO no matter how many inmates are out there," said County Treasurer Linda Clark, who bemoaned the multiple riots and the millions paid. County Auditor Lynn Owens observed that GEO has never received a merit-based increase in federal per diem payments, and both officials agreed that the county should be in charge at the Detention Center.

The prison industry occasionally runs into resident opposition of the not-in-my-backyard sort. In Otero County, residents of Alamogordo blocked a proposed GEO immigrant prison because the intended site was within the city limits. Several years later, a new proposal from MTC for a USMS immigrant prison 70 miles away on the far south side of the county was approved by the Otero County Commission with little protest. The county liked the business—a half-dollar a day per immigrant in the 630-bed prison—so much that it signed on with

MTC in 2008 to build an ICE-fed, 1,100-bed detention center next to the existing prison.

Poverty partly explains the willingness to scrape a couple of dollars off federal per diem payments and in the process incur massive bond debt. The prison industry introduces the governments of desperate communities to what some call "backdoor financing": project revenue bonds in the tens of millions of dollars that suddenly make them feel like economic players.

Since funding is provided by project revenue bonds rather than general obligation bonds, the county faces no direct liability if the speculative prison fails. "Money for nothing" is a common refrain when county officers are asked about the advisability of prison deals. This answer, however, is as naïve as it sounds. Even though the bondholders cannot hold the issuing government responsible if the speculative prison fails, there are still real costs, as Reeves County is experiencing. Responding to legal complaints and paying financial advisors is a burden, and lower bond ratings increase the costs of all new bonds. The county's overall bond rating was down-graded to a highly speculative level in 2003 when the prison expansion resulted in an empty complex. GEO eventually stepped in to negotiate a deal with BOP for more inmates.

Reeves was hit with a $45 million-plus reconstruction bill after the inmate disturbances, and to cover all its bills the county restructured existing prison bonds and issued $19.7 million in new revenue bonds in 2010 to pay for repairs and upgrades not covered by insurance. Now that Reeves has collected damages for its prison property, it also pays higher insurance premiums.

The full cost of the public-private immigrant prisons that now litter the Southwest and elsewhere is not yet known. Most counties and municipalities are still ten to fifteen years away from paying off the bonds. But poor rural governments worried that they may have been snookered into the prison business have some options. Last year Haskell County, Texas, sold its Rolling Plains Regional Jail & Detention Center for immigrants to the Inland Real Estate Group, a Chicago-based holding company specializing in shopping malls and government properties.

## Governing Through Crime

Beyond the false hopes and corporate greed that build immigrant prisons, their expansion, like that of other prisons that have mushroomed across the rural United States, seems fueled by something both sinister and uniquely American. The growing divide between citizens and immigrants is only partially responsible for what has befallen this new class of inmates. A wider sensibility about prisoners is also at work. The men and women held behind the perimeter fences are never seen, never discussed. The prison is treated as a waste dump, similarly placed on the community's edge, where property values are low and there are no neighbors. The prisoners themselves are society's refuse, its discards, outcasts, and outsiders who have lost their membership rights in the human community.

The United States's high incarceration rate—fives times greater than the average rate in the rest of the world—is evidence, says Virginia Democratic Senator Jim Webb, that we are "doing something dramatically wrong in our criminal justice system." Senator Webb apparently saw no contradiction in advocating an end to mass incarceration while supporting an amendment to the 2007 Homeland Security Appropriations bill calling for a 50% increase in the number of immigrant-detention beds, increased criminal penalties and mandatory minimum prison sentences for those like Galindo who reenter the country without authorization, and strengthened criminal alien laws that would result in deportation for drug violations and other so-called "aggravated felonies."

Since the 1970s crime control has become a central theme in U.S. politics and society. In the words of Berkeley Law professor Jonathan Simon, we are "governing through crime": isolation and exclusion in an expansive penal system is the dominant response to tough social problems. Although the immigrant crackdown raises its own special concerns, it largely mirrors and merges with the broader wars on drugs and crime in terms of increasing costs, expanding law enforcement, high incarceration rates, and dismal cost-benefit ratios. Immigration, a contentious social issue lacking any easy policy solution, has similarly been addressed through increased enforcement and incarceration.

Given that get-tough models are the basis for our current approach to immigration, it comes as little surprise that, like the war on crime, the immigrant crackdown has flooded the federal courts with nonviolent offenders, besieged poor communities, and dramatically increased the U.S. prison population, while doing little to solve the problem itself.

## Bipartisan Crackdown

Enforcement practices such as Operation Streamline (and its many cousins: Operation Jump Start, Operation Return-to-Sender, Operation Reservation Guaranteed) and such absurdities as the border wall are not the partisan initiatives of restrictionist forces in Congress. The post-9/11 commitments by DHS to "protect America against dangerous people and goods" and to "restore respect for immigration laws" by making immigration enforcement and border patrol "consistent" and "comprehensive" are central to the immigration positions of both major political parties. Indeed, it has been Democrats, such as U.S. Representative David Price of North Carolina, who have led the efforts to extend Operation Streamline and pursue criminal aliens. Visiting Del Rio, Price, former chair of the Homeland Security Subcommittee of the House Appropriations Committee, gushed, "It's just a great model we need to put to use everywhere."

What the Bush administration started with ICE's reinforced Criminal Alien Program, the Obama administration further institutionalized and expanded. While the Border Patrol, through Operation Streamline, greatly expanded the population of criminal aliens by prosecuting masses of illegal border crossers for the first time, ICE created a new stream of criminal aliens by vastly expanding the role of local law enforcement in immigration enforcement through Secure Communities and the 287(g) program. For the Obama administration and the Democratic Party, the invigorated targeting of criminal aliens was not only virtuous—focusing on criminal immigrants rather than on otherwise noncriminal illegal immigrants—but was also politically attractive given the broad political consensus that immigrants who are criminals have no rightful place in American society. What is more, proponents of reform—such as President Obama—that would legalize the immense unauthorized immigrant population could point to the rigorous campaign against criminal aliens as evidence of their commitment to upholding the rule of law.

But by expanding the dragnet to catch more and more immigrants, the Obama administration has contributed to the misperception that immigrants are disproportionately responsible for crime. A quick review of the increase in federal criminal prosecutions in the Southwest during the first two years of the Obama administration underscores the common perception that immigration and crime are closely linked.

Less than 10 percent of the nation's population lives in the five federal districts along the southwestern border—Arizona, the Southern District of California (San Diego), New Mexico, the Western District of Texas (San Antonio), and the Southern District of Texas (Houston)—yet in 2010 47 percent of federal felony prosecutions occurred there, up from 36 percent in 2007. In its annual budget proposals, the U.S. Marshals Service pleads for large budget increases to cope with the dramatic rise in immigrants in custody. On any given day, more than 40 percent of the inmates in USMS detention centers are immigrants.

Deportations are up, too. In 2010 ICE removed 195,772 criminal aliens—up 52.5 percent over 2009. More than half of the 392,000 immigrants deported in 2010 were criminal aliens.

These numbers suggest an alarming level of criminality among illegal immigrants, but a closer looks reveals a more sober reality, one that nonetheless put

Jesus Galindo on the path to his tragic death in a privately run federal prison. Between 2007 and 2010 felony immigration prosecutions in the Southwest increased 77 percent, and non-felony immigration prosecutions in the same five federal districts jumped by 259 percent. Despite ICE's assertions that it targets the most dangerous criminal aliens, even those immigrants convicted only of illegal entry are labeled criminal aliens. The campaign to remove all criminal aliens from the country extends beyond illegal immigrants to legal immigrants, whose past or present convictions for drug violations come to the attention of ICE. More than 44,000 of the immigrants—many of them convicted of drug-possession charges, usually marijuana, while present legally—deported by ICE in 2010 were designated criminal aliens due to what the agency calls "dangerous drugs" charges.

By 2010 the immigrant crackdown had achieved unprecedented scope. This despite a steady decline in the number of immigrants crossing the southwestern border illegally. Whereas 1.1 million crossed in 2005, that number fell to 444,500 in 2010. Meanwhile, ICE aims to have its Secure Communities program deputizing local law enforcement nationwide by 2013.

In the third year of the Obama administration, the largely unregulated archipelago of immigrant prisons looks much as it did when he took office, although there have been small signs of improvement in ICE's sprawling network of detention centers.

In the summer of 2009 ICE announced a "major overhaul" of the detention system, including the creation of an Office of Detention Planning and Policy. However, while committing the agency to increased oversight of the more than 350 facilities where immigrants are held for processing and deportation, ICE director John Morton said the number of detainees would not decrease and the agency had no plans to end its relationships with its many partners in state and local government or with private prison contractors. Morton refused to support legally binding and enforceable minimum standards for immigrant-detention centers, sorely disappointing immigrant-rights and prison-reform advocates. Two years later immigrant advocates have applauded the steps taken to increase oversight, but say that despite the placement of ICE "detention managers" in contracted detention centers, human rights abuses continue.

There's even less light, reason, concern, or justice in the "criminal" realm of the immigrant-prison archipelago. The Obama administration has maintained the complex of immigrant-only USMS and BOP prisons hidden in the shadows of our country's immigration and criminal justice systems. The "privatization management" divisions of both USMS and BOP are doing a brisk business, issuing dozens of new contracts in the past few years to private-prison companies and their local-government enablers. Even Reeves County—following its two prison riots, the lawsuit protesting wrongful deaths, and complaints within BOP about deficiencies at the prison—had it contracts renewed.

The Obama administration has deftly deflected ethical arguments against mass detention with liberal rule-of-law logic. DHS, it argues, is simply upholding the rule of law by consistently and wholeheartedly enforcing immigration statutes and securing the border. (Though DHS and DOJ have stopped some high-profile individual deportations, thereby contradicting the administration's claims.) Rather than echoing or shadowing the ideological restrictionism of the right, as the Bush administration did, the Obama administration argues that enforcement-first immigration policy will establish the political foundation for immigration reform. But there is no sign yet that the administration or the Democratic leadership are willing to lead the way toward durable immigration reform that would address both the future structure of immigration and the failures of the existing immigration system.

Such a reform should be based on measurements of how immigration flows affect existing wages. Armed with these benchmarks, we can establish how much new immigration is sustainable. The goal is both to ensure that new immigration will not undermine wages or working conditions in the U.S. labor force, and, at the same time, to allow American society and the economy to benefit from regulated flows of unskilled and skilled labor. Reforms would need to account for unauthorized immigrants who for many years were tolerated or even welcomed in the United States. These immigrants and their families have integrated into this country, and should now be accorded a path to citizenship.

As the immigrant crackdown continues, hundreds of thousands of immigrants like Jesus Manuel Galindo will be caught in the profit-driven public-private-prison complex. In the end though, the human cost of the system is unlikely to bring it down. It may only be when citizens and politicians start questioning the financial cost of incarcerating immigrants that these public-private prisons will go bust.

**Article of Faith**

Not much has changed in Pecos since the mid-1980s, when Reeves County hitched its future to America's hardening criminal justice system and booming prison industry.

Today, the median price of occupied housing in Reeves is $29,400, the lowest of any county in the United States. Nearly one-third of the county's families live in poverty. The county government, similarly, is in desperate straits. In the wake of the prison riots, the county was forced to kill a $16-million bond issuance to build a new library and community recreational facility.

Yet no one here questions—publicly, at least—the conventional wisdom that the Reeves County Detention Center has been good for Pecos and the county. Twenty-five years after the prison opened, the people of Pecos still believe that their future is inextricably linked to the prison.

It's not that the residents of Pecos are proud to live in a prison town. But there is no shame either—even after Galindo's death and the riots. The locals know that if the flow of immigrant inmates dry up, the town will die. At a county commissioners' meeting following the riots, County Attorney Alvarez bluntly summed up the community's economic dependence on imprisoned immigrants: "Without that prison, basically, Reeves County is going under."

Alavarez need not be too concerned. Despite an array of legal complaints against the county, GEO, PNA, and BOP, only the rioters have been held responsible. The U.S. Attorney pressed charges against 26 inmates identified by GEO as having been involved. They were convicted and sentenced to an additional year in detention. After the initial April 2009 count against them failed to elicit guilty pleas— there was little hard evidence—the U.S. Attorney's office added another count to the indictment under an obscure statute requiring a mandatory ten-year sentence for the use of fire in the commission of a federal crime. Under threat, all pled guilty to the first charge. A wary GEO demanded the county erect an elaborate system of surveillance cameras in the prison. Meanwhile BOP has dispersed to other private prisons those allegedly involved in the two disturbances, and more than a hundred inmates are being prosecuted for involvement in the second riot.

After the riots Barry Friedman, the Dallas bondsman who brokered the county's first prison bonds in 1985, came to the rescue with a plan to refinance the existing prison debt and sell nearly $20 million in new revenue bonds to cover prison reconstruction expenses. Friedman's company, Carlyle Capital Markets, has structured and sold $170 million in prison bonds for Reeves County since 1985. Freidman receives healthy commissions from the bond sales and took in $15,000 per month to help Reeves sort its way out of the post-rioting financial crisis.

Through the miracles of debt financing and speculative investment, the crisis has stabilized. Reeves's annual debt-service payments are only a million dollars higher—rising to $14.5 million—than they were before the riots. The relieved Commissioners Court is unfazed by the knowledge that in just two years it will have to pay an additional $5 million in debt servicing. Nor is there much apparent concern over the fact that a prison complex valued at $89 million required a principal debt of $100.5 million and will cost $135.8 million in debt servicing. By the time the county assumes full ownership of the prison—2021, according to the current schedule—its BOP contracts will be long gone.

The Privatization Management Branch, the BOP division that handles the twelve privately operated criminal-alien prisons (including five in West Texas), was similarly unperturbed by the prison riots. Although several hundred inmates were removed during reconstruction, BOP quickly returned them and even raised its rate of payment. According to GEO's Warden Dwight Sims, BOP was "impressed with the control of the inmates."

With the new financing in place, the prison complex reconstructed with an infirmary, and BOP contracts unaffected, America's largest immigrant prison is once again up and running. The 2010 prison-bonds certificate is replete with statistics on immigration enforcement and increased rates of federal imprisonment. Aiming to assure bondholders and Bank of New York Mellon Trust, who've invested in Reeves's poorly rated (B and BBB-) instruments, the certificate points to a continuing strong "demand" by BOP for privately operated prison facilities that supply the increasing "market" for the housing of criminal aliens.

In his unsuccessful 2010 campaign for reelection, former County Judge Contreras pointed to the more than 500 jobs supplied by the prison complex, noting, "We have earned a profit which will help reduce taxes for Reeves County residents." Meanwhile, his opponent and eventual successor, W.J. Bang, told prospective voters that he foresees a time when prison profits will enable the county to "eliminate its property tax altogether."

Two and a half decades after Reeves County launched the private prison business, faith in the financial possibilities of immigrant imprisonment still abounds.

# 2

*At War in Texas*

HEADS BOWED IN PRAYER, WE STAND AT A BU-
colic spot on the banks of the Rio Grande known by
locals as Neely's Crossing. Like most of West Texas,
there is nothing here. On the other side, drug wars
have turned Mexican border towns in the Valle de
Juárez and elsewhere into killing grounds.

As Hudspeth County deputies armed with AR-
15 semi-automatic weapons stand guard, we close in
around Reverend Jim Garlow. "Lord, we thank you
Lord for gathering us here," he says. "We thank you
for all you have given us and our great nation. We
ask you Lord to protect American exceptionalism,
to protect U.S. national sovereignty, and secure our
border." Garlow, a prominent evangelical minister,

recently had been selected by former House Speaker Newt Gingrich to serve as chairman of Renewing American Leadership (ReAL), a new organization dedicated to promoting the "'otherness' of America's exceptional culture and government [whose] manifest success . . . . has made us a target."

Garlow was speaking to the attendees at a two-day "Border School" sponsored by the Border Sheriff's Posse, an evangelical group that teams up with the Texas Border Sheriff's Coalition (TBSC) and the Southwestern Border Sheriff's Coalition to educate Christians about threats some law enforcement officials believe loom across the border.

Neely's Crossing became famous for a January 23, 2006 incident that Hudspeth sheriff and TBSC chairman Arvin West contends was a "Mexican military incursion." The day before we visited the site, we viewed blurry footage of heavily armed men scrambling across the river toward the Mexican side. Several loads of marijuana float downriver as the men try to regroup and get a military-like vehicle, a Hummer or possibly Humvee, back onto Mexican soil. The Mexican government vehemently denied Sheriff West's accusation that a Mexican military unit had been escorting drug smugglers. The Border Patrol, which had officers at Neely's Crossing that day, declined to support West's account.

Claiming that the federal government has abandoned its border-control responsibilities, West, who is a mainstay of the Border School, warns students and residents of U.S. border communities, "Arm yourselves. It's better to be tried by twelve than carried by six."

This secure-the-line-at-all-costs attitude doesn't merely foster right-wing ranting. West and other border sheriffs tout border security lore such as the Neely's Crossing incident in congressional testimony, and Fox News often reports their assertions. The complaints that Washington isn't fulfilling its responsibilities echo across border communities, despite the unprecedented increase over the past five years in the number of Border Patrol agents, immigrant-detention beds, and border barriers. Each year, billions of dollars flow to the border from the Departments of Homeland Security (DHS) and Justice (DOJ).

While there is little validity to complaints about the lack of federal funds for border security, the criticism about federal irresponsibility on border policy conveys an important truth. Since 9/11, the border has become a site of intensive national concern, not only surrounding immigration, but also drug wars and terrorism. In this context of increasing fear, the federal government has failed to assess the threats and address them coherently.

Instead, Washington has fed opportunistic local and state officials who use federal grants to shape the politics and operations of border security. There may be no cogent federal stance on border policy, but there is policy—dictated by alarmist border-area sheriffs and politicians and increasingly supported by the American public, Congress, and the Obama administration. To that end, the federal government is busy resurrecting discredited drug-war programs, deploying the National Guard, and opening new channels of assistance for border security by redirecting stimulus grants that were intended to repair the wider U.S. economy.

## The Texas Paradigm

Nowhere has the post-9/11 border security framework been so enthusiastically adopted—and adapted—as in Texas, where local law enforcement, the state political leadership, and a contingent of the congressional delegation have taken border security into their own hands, albeit largely with federal funding.

The shaping of what Governor Rick Perry calls the "Texas model of border security" began in the spring of 2005, when Zapata County Sheriff Sigifredo "Sigi" Gonzalez, Jr. put out a call to his fellow Texas-border sheriffs to form the Texas Border Sheriff's Coalition, which includes twenty border counties. Over the past five years, the sheriffs of the TBSC have rallied law enforcement to secure the border, played a prominent role in the state's "high-intensity border surges," and launched Border Watch, a remote-surveillance program carried out by volunteer "virtual deputies." In the process, the sheriffs have become the public face of Texas's go-it-alone commitment to border security. We are the "can-do state," Gonzalez says.

In PowerPoint presentations, congressional testimony, and media interviews, Gonzalez warns of al Qaeda terrorists setting up sleeper cells, Mexican drug cartels crisscrossing the border to terrorize U.S. communities, and ominous flyovers by the black helicopters of the Mexican army. His frustration at the perceived "inadequacy of our federal government to protect our border in preventing a potential terrorist and their weapons of mass destruction from entering our country" spurred him to organize the TBSC in 2005. Two years later he founded the Southwestern Border Sheriff's Coalition.

As any Texas-border sheriff will tell you, "Operation Linebacker" is the tactical core of the state's model. If a terrorist, criminal alien, drug smuggler, or illegal border crosser makes it through the Border Patrol's frontline, the linebackers—sheriffs and their deputies—are there to make the tackle. In a state where football is a barely secular religion, the analogy captures hearts and minds. It also conveniently complements the federal government's own structure of local-federal cooperation in immigration and border enforcement, thereby facilitating the flow of DHS and DOJ funding. At the same time, though, most border sheriffs insist that their departments actually are ahead of the feds, a posture repeatedly underscored by Governor Perry, who calls the border sheriffs the state's "first line of defense."

Perry quickly allied himself with the TBSC. He gave it funds from the governor's Criminal Justice Division and launched an umbrella border security program called Operation Border Star. Together, Operations Linebacker and Border Star were integrated into the state's homeland security apparatus, which Perry and Homeland Security Office Director Steve

McCraw began assembling in 2004 with DHS grants. McCraw is a tight-jawed, no-nonsense former FBI officer, who now heads Texas's Department of Public Safety (DPS) while continuing his duties at the Homeland Security Office. "Texas," he boasts, "has created a new paradigm for border security, and the Border Patrol is now adopting parts of it."

McCraw and Perry summarize that paradigm with an oft-repeated maxim: "There can be no homeland security without border security." As outlined in the state's Homeland Security Strategic Plan 2010–2015, the model is designed to "prevent terrorists and criminal enterprises from exploiting Texas' international borders, including land, air, and sea."

Border Star, a main vehicle for the Texas paradigm, is more than boots on the ground. Encouraged by DHS's call for locally networked information-gathering—and by infusions of DHS and DOJ dollars—the governor's office directed the creation of intelligence and "fusion" centers that bring together law enforcement agencies. McCraw has put his stamp on Border Star through such high-tech information-gathering initiatives as the Texas Data Exchange Program (TDEx) and the TxMap crime-mapping project, as well as through the Border Security and Operations Center (BSOC) in Austin and the six Joint Intelligence and Operations Centers (JOIC), four of which are housed in the headquarters of Border Patrol sectors and work together with the Border Patrol's Border Intelligence Centers. The most recent additions to Border Star's stable are the Unified Commands, which serve as a network for law enforcement agencies in 45 counties of the borderland region.

The latest tweaking of the state's border security model came in September 2009, during Perry's reelection campaign. He announced that the Texas Rangers would begin the Ranger Recon mission along the border. The Texas Rangers, formed in the early 1880s to protect the Republic of Texas against Mexico and to subdue the Cherokees, is the DPS agency that nominally oversees BSOC, the border JOICs, and other border security operations.

The Texas border security model is not home-grown. It is largely outsourced to an Arlington, Virginia consulting firm, Abrams Learning & Information Systems (ALIS). Texas has contracted with ALIS to direct and staff most of the state's border security operations. Over the past three years, under the directorship of Steve McCraw, DPS has paid ALIS nearly $20 million in state and federal funds to "refine plans and strategies for seamless integration of border security operations in the State of Texas." As part of its multiple contracts, ALIS has also been charged with formulating the Texas Border Security Campaign Plan, Homeland Security Strategic Plan 2010–2015, and the TEXDPS Agency Strategy Plan 2010. Not only does ALIS formulate the state's border security model, it has also been charged with coordinating and overseeing many of the Border Star operations, including BSOC, the JOICs, TDEx, TxMap, and the Unified Commands.

In the can-do state, there's a can-do attitude about border security, not found elsewhere. "Is it really possible to seal the 1,200-mile Texas border?" I ask McCraw. It's a question I often ask, and most border security practitioners and observers respond that the borderlands are too immense and too remote to control completely. But McCraw doesn't equivocate. "We can secure the border in Texas with enough resources," he answers without hesitation. Sheriff West is equally confident about his ability to secure Hudspeth County. "Just give me 75 more deputies, armed with AR-15s or AK-47s, enough trucks and ATVs, and we can shut the border down," he told me.

McCraw says he is committed to "secur[ing] the border for Texans," and he and the governor think other states and DHS should follow their lead. In February 2009 Governor Perry wrote to DHS Secretary Janet Napolitano to invite her to observe Operation Border Star, so that she "might consider this approach as a national model to increase border security."

It's unclear what Perry and McCraw would show Napolitano other than the enthusiasm with which state and border law enforcement have jumped on the border security bandwagon. From the start the Texas paradigm has been hounded by public-relations scandals, widespread skepticism about reputed results, and charges of power-grabbing and political opportunism. Soon after the sheriffs launched Operation Linebacker, their increased patrols and traffic checkpoints were met with indignation and outrage. Residents complained that checkpoints instituted by then-sheriff Leo Samaniego in the El Paso area functioned as a dragnet for illegal immigrants and led to few arrests of criminals who could be regarded as a threat to community safety, let alone homeland security. The series of border "surges"—beginning in January 2006 with another football-themed program, Operation Free Safety—were initially accompanied by great fanfare orchestrated by Perry's office but have since been abandoned after they came under repeated fire. In Austin and non-border areas of the state, legislators and residents were concerned that public-safety resources were being used for political purposes. A review last year by a state commission found that the diversion of state troopers under Border Star contributed to DPS's "critical personnel shortage, weakening its ability to protect the public." Meanwhile border residents, including some of the sheriffs, complain that the state troopers gave out more traffic tickets but arrested no major drug runners.

Some of the most severe criticism of the Texas border security paradigm has come from within state government. Perry's border security operations, while now directed from McCraw's base at DPS, originated in the governor's Homeland Security Office and the associated Governor's Department of Emergency Management (GDEM). This created tensions and major communications gaps with DPS, which regarded some of the new homeland and border security projects as duplications of their efforts.

A July 2009 report by the state legislature's Sunset Advisory Commission recognized this problem, concluding, "Lines of authority between DPS, GDEM, and the Governor's Office of Homeland Security are unclear." To remedy that problem, DPS took over GDEM, whose name was changed to the Texas Department of Emergency Management. Those tensions and communications problems between the governor's office and DPS dissipated when Perry replaced the DPS director last year with his own man, Steve McCraw.

Along with the patrolling methods, Border Star's information-technology systems also have come under scrutiny. An April 2007 article in the *Texas Observer*, described the Data Exchange program run by ALIS as "a headlong pursuit of control through information hoarding for a project in search of a purpose." "Money has been squandered," the article contended, "sensitive data potentially lost, and security warnings unheeded." In a March 2009 study, *Operation Border Star: Wasted Millions and Missed Opportunities*, the Texas ACLU concluded that the

> recent development of a vast regional network of fusion centers and 'Joint Operations Intelligence Centers' are not serving the goal of public safety and confus-

ing valuable criminal intelligence with unimportant statistics and innocent activities.

At an April 29, 2010 legislative hearing in the booming city of McAllen (the border twin of Reynosa, Mexico), Texas ACLU director Terri Burke argued that the governor's model of border security is "making Texans poorer, not safer." More often the main result of the stepped-up patrols, she said, is the "inconvenience or harassment of law-abiding individuals, not the apprehension of violent criminals." The ACLU's review of Border Star found that rather than targeted surges, the governor's border security operations were indiscriminate sweeps. Some communities had more traffic stops than residents. Border Star, Burke added, has "done little if anything to interrupt the violent business of transnational drug smugglers and human traffickers." No information offered by Perry or McCraw in their strategy statements, budget proposals for Border Star, legislative testimony, or campaign ads disputes that assessment.

During a three-week "border surge operation" in mid-2006, ALIS Vice-President Leo Rios, told reporters, without any supporting documentation, that the surge demonstrated that "we're capable of shutting down all transports of illegal drugs and criminals in this area to zero for up to seven days." Rios touted the company's role in Texas border security operations at a homeland security technology conference in Washington last October, and credited ALIS's innovative TxMap crime-mapping system with its supposedly stellar results. Who can doubt that on the border there is no difference between the war on drugs and homeland security? Even those responsible refuse to differentiate.

The Texas paradigm of border security has been subject to the same sharp criticisms as the homeland- and border security projects of DHS. Accusations of waste, dysfunction, duplication, absence of oversight, over-reliance on private contractors, and lack of direction are common. Meanwhile, tangible security improvements are nearly impossible to find. Border security in Texas is less the model for DHS that Perry brags about than a mirror of the federal government's own willy-nilly implementation of border security.

## Stimulating Security

In Texas, can-do confidence often is paired with arrogant go-it-alone posturing. That bluster was on display at a Tea Party rally in Austin on tax day in 2009, when Governor Rick Perry warned that Texas might once again secede from the Union, as it had in 1861. Earlier that year the governor rallied Tea Partiers by joining a chorus of Republican governors threatening to reject all or part of the Obama administration's stimulus package for the states. Threats aside, Perry did, of course, accept funding from the American Recovery and Reinvestment Act (ARRA)—tens of millions of dollars of which are being used to underwrite Border Star.

Even so, Perry continues to boast of the state's steadfast and solitary commitment to secure its border. In a 2010 campaign ad, Perry, who was running for his third term, declared, "If Washington won't protect our border, Texas will. Here along the Rio Grande we're funding a border-wide crime control effort, led by local enforcement." The ad features video of him walking with sheriff's deputies on the banks of the river. This is an enduring theme. In a 2006 campaign ad, Sheriff Gonzalez attested, "When local law enforcement needed help protecting the border, Governor Perry was the only one who answered the call and delivered the resources needed to help us."

Perry's campaign ads never mention the fundamental role played by federal funds in launching and expanding Border Star and other state-directed border security projects. This year's infusion of ARRA stimulus dollars, which has given the Texas-border sheriffs and Border Star programs an extra boost, is only the latest example. Federal funds have underwritten local and state border security operations in Texas since 2004.

Grants from DHS began flowing to the state soon after the creation of the Department in 2003, establishing the foundation for the Texas paradigm. It wasn't until fiscal year 2007 that Perry finally succeeded in persuading the state legislature to kick in about $50 million annually for Border Star, although that funding is now being eaten up by the state's financial crisis, and additional state funding for border security is not likely to materialize.

Virtually all state-directed homeland security programs to protect against terrorism and to secure the border are funded by DHS. Border counties in Texas receive about $20 million annually in DHS grants funneled through the governor's office. In addition, DHS's Operation Stonegarden provides the governor with an annual grant—$17.5 million in 2010—to be distributed to border law enforcement for its Operation Linebacker patrols.

Yet, for all of Homeland Security's largesse, it is the Justice Department that has been most instrumental in paying for Texas's border security strategy. Starting in 2005 Perry began channeling DOJ funds from his office—through its Criminal Justice Division, Homeland Security Office, and Department of Emergency Management—to the TBSC, DPS, and border law enforcement agencies. Also in 2005 the TBSC began receiving a $4.5–$5 million annual congressional earmark via the DOJ's Bureau of Justice Assistance. The Coalition uses the funds to pay Operation Linebacker overtime salaries and to buy equipment.

DOJ criminal justice grants have been the silent partner in the state's border security campaign. From January 2006 through April 2010, the governor's Criminal Justice Division dedicated $99.4 million for border security initiatives, $80.1 million of which came from DOJ grants, including $39.5 million ARRA dollars.

That $39.5 million is a portion of a $90.3-million ARRA grant to the Criminal Justice Division, which, according to the governor's office, provides "the unique opportunity to strengthen the foundation of the criminal justice system in Texas by equipping agencies and communities with resources to enhance public safety."

Yet the distribution of nearly half of this ARRA funding to the governor's dubious border security initiatives underscores the contention that large sums of recovery funding are being used for pork-barrel projects to court political patronage. That contention is further supported by the fantastical claims that border sheriffs make in order to obtain the money.

For instance, the Hudspeth County Sheriff's Department, in its approved application for $415,000 in stimulus funds, proposed that a state-directed ARRA grant would enable County deputies to continue progress begun under Operation Linebacker in "responding to criminal activity, narcoterrorism, human trafficking, and the brutal crimes associated with sophisticated and organized criminal enterprises." The proposal's account of border security threats includes Sheriff West's assertion that "the Mexican military crossed into Hudspeth County to protect smugglers [*sic*] marijuana."

During one of my visits to West's office, the sheriff launched into a story of how Venezuelan President

Hugo Chávez is training the drug cartels in terrorist tactics with the assistance and financing of al Qaeda. And during a break at the May 2010 TBSC meeting, Deputy Robert Wilson, Hudspeth's grant-writer, solemnly reported that there are Middle Eastern terrorists on the border. "We know they are coming through," he said. If that isn't enough to get you terrified about border security, Wilson is convinced that there are Chinese soldiers—and Russians, too—immersing themselves in the Mexican population; one day they will "just put on their uniforms and come north." Sheriff West, with his homespun style, silver tongue, and storyteller's bravado, leaves you wondering how much of these border security tales he actually believes, though he is only too happy to collect the federal money they attract.

The reliability of the supporting statistics in the ARRA grant applications is as questionable as the stories of terrorists on the border and Mexican military drug-running incursions. Hudspeth County reported that a previous DOJ grant enabled it to make 176 felony arrests and 176 felony convictions—an amazing performance by the county attorney. West hopes to best that record under the ARRA grant, which projects 200 arrests and 200 convictions for 2010. In its ARRA application to the governor's office, the sheriff's department claimed that an internal review of its Operation Linebacker patrols "revealed that . . . the use of additional law enforcement resources in Hudspeth County prevent[ed] terrorist activities" and "resulted in a decrease in local crime rates by as much as 78%." This is a county where incidences of violent crime are measured in the single digits and population is steadily declining.

The pork likely is flowing not only from the DOJ via Perry's Criminal Justice Division, but from the federal government directly. Texas law enforcement agencies are tapping a new DOJ criminal justice program created by ARRA stimulus funds, the State and Local Law Enforcement Assistance Program: Combating Criminal Narcotics Activity Stemming from the Southern Border of the United States. Some grantees have used funding to channel drug users into treatment programs, but most follow the traditional drug-war practice of arresting and imprisoning drug users and street dealers.

Performance metrics are also drug-war standard issue: number of drug seizures, vehicle seizures, arrests, and sentenced inmates. In Cameron County, at Texas's extreme southern tip, deputies of the newly created Special Investigations Unit are busy stuffing a hanger with high-value vehicles seized in drug busts. So successful is the new undercover narc unit that the department's evidence room is now packed full with marijuana, and new seizures have to be stored in a large metal container outside the building.

One of the givens of the drug war at home and abroad is that drug enforcement breeds corruption. Since 1994 four South Texas sheriffs have been convicted of drug-related corruption. One of the more recent cases is former Cameron County Sheriff Conrado Cantu, who is serving a 24-year sentence for using his office to extort money from drug offenders. Just west of Cameron County, in the Rio Grande Valley, former Sheriff Reymundo "Rey" Guerra of Starr County is serving a 64-month sentence after being convicted last year of facilitating Gulf Cartel drug trafficking through his jurisdiction.

Despite this recent history, Cameron County's current sheriff, Omar Lucio, won a $2.2 million counter-narcotics grant to fund the new twelve-person Special Investigations Unit to "combat drug and arms trafficking along the border and reduce money laundering, drug-related crime, and community violence." Lucio calls the new narcotics campaign Operation Border Eagle. According to the Cameron County Sheriff's Department, since the implementation of Border Eagle, the monthly average arrest rate increased from ten to 29 and the vehicle-seizure rate from three to six. Border Eagle develops twenty narcotics cases a month, up from the six the Department generated before ARRA funding kicked in. With regard to arms trafficking, there is no progress report, but the sheriff did tell the federal Bureau of Justice Assistance that the number of handguns seized each month by the narcotics unit increased from one to three.

According to available evidence, increased border security, like the failed war on drugs, has not made illicit drugs less accessible. The market for illegal drugs entering the country from Mexico involves 25 million Americans. And, as border security operations intensify, the National Drug Intelligence Center warns, "the overall threat posed by illicit drugs will not diminish in the near term."

These days border sheriffs routinely count on at least two and often three or four sources of funding for overtime border patrolling. Caught up in the alleged urgency of supporting border sheriffs, no one—not DHS, not DOJ, not Congress, and not states' homeland security offices that distribute these grants—is evaluating the impact of this aid on border law enforcement. There are accounting audits of individual grants, but no agency is watching for double-dipping, whereby law enforcement organs receive money from multiple sources for the same purpose.

Faced with unprecedented sums of federal funding, many rural sheriffs' departments have been forced to hire grant administrators to handle the paperwork. But the sheriffs have few complaints—other than that they deserve still more money, especially to pay for full-time employees rather than overtime for deputies. Sparsely inhabited Hudspeth County—just 3,058 inhabitants; 0.7 per square mile—is awash in federal border security funding. The county, which has an annual budget of about $5 million, receives as much as $1 million per year in border security grants. In Zapata County, Sheriff Gonzalez has so much border security funding from DHS and DOJ that each of his deputies is assigned two vehicles, a patrol car for regular duty and a new SUV for overtime border security operations.

The ballooning budgets of the sheriffs departments are the envy of the commissioners in Texas's rural, border-area counties, sixteen of which are among the hundred poorest counties in the United States. Border sheriffs enjoy virtually unlimited overtime-pay accounts, new fleets of vehicles, and the latest security technology. Meanwhile, commissioners watch helplessly as county revenues sink because of declining populations and stagnating local economies, as social services and schools plunge into decrepitude.

## Drug War Dinosaur

"Border security" is a flexible policy framework that comfortably accommodates crackdowns on crime, immigrants, and drugs. Enforcement areas have merged both rhetorically and in practice. Thus the DOJ criminal justice grants that fund border security operations in Texas are based on a two-decade-old federal program to prop up the criminal justice systems of states and localities fighting the war on drugs.

Congress created the Byrne Memorial and Local Law Enforcement Grant Program (named after a New York police officer murdered by drug-gang members) as part of the Anti-Drug Abuse Act of 1988. Though the Program, renamed the Byrne Justice Assistance Grant in 2005, was established during the Reagan administration, Democrats, notably Joe Biden, have been its staunchest supporters. In 1988—with Michael Dukakis as the party's less-than-ruthless standard-bearer in the presidential election—Democrats in Congress were especially eager to brandish the party's tough-on-crime, tougher-on-drugs principles. In the mid-1990s Byrne funding rose to and stayed at about $1 billion annually, driven by a convergence of political enthusiasm for drug enforcement, President Clinton's appeal to law enforcement and crime-crackdown constituencies, and the emergence of an anti-immigrant backlash in Congress.

Although Byrne grants to the states (which get 60 percent of annual appropriations) and localities can be used for a variety of public-safety and criminal justice programs, historically they have been deployed to fight the drug war at home, mainly through the creation and maintenance of regional drug task forces and local counter-narcotics units.

Nine of every ten Byrne dollars that flowed from Washington to Austin in the 1990s supported these counter-narcotics teams. Undercover narcs and allied prosecutors in small towns in Texas mounted aggressive (and criminal) campaigns to round up the usual suspects—mainly African Americans. Perhaps the most notorious case was the arrest in 1999 of 46 mostly African American Tulia residents on drug charges based on the perjured testimony of gypsy cop Tom Coleman—named "Lawman of the Year" by then–Texas Attorney General John Cornyn. Currently serving as the state's junior senator, Cornyn is a strong proponent of the entire range of border security programs and is the highly esteemed friend of the state's rural border sheriffs.

The persistence and support of legal-advocacy groups such as the ACLU and Texas Criminal Justice Coalition and progressive groups such as the Drug Policy Alliance and the NAACP helped expose the pervasive corruption, waste, and civil rights violations involved in counter-narcotics operations both in Texas and in the country at large. But it was criticism leveled at the Byrne funds by conservative organizations such as the National Taxpayers Union and the Heritage Foundation—that the grants were wasteful and furthered federal intervention in state and local affairs—that precipitated President George W. Bush's 2005 decision to cut $940 million from federal-assistance programs that were "not able to effectively demonstrate an impact on reducing crime."

At the border, however, growing national concerns about the high cost of incarceration, the futility of the drug war, and the over-federalization of the criminal justice and law enforcement systems all fade. The language of border control collapses and intensifies a continuum of threats: illegal border crossers merge seamlessly with illegal drug users, criminal aliens, marijuana backpackers, transnational gangs, drug-trafficking organizations, narcoterrorists, smuggled weapons of mass destruction, and jihadists. And the Obama administration has responded as though the rhetoric matches reality.

Obama's preferred vehicle has been the Byrne program. Byrne grants to California, Arizona, New Mexico, and Texas dropped from $100.9 million in 2005 to $34.7 million in 2008. Under Obama, the trend has reversed; Byrne funding to the four southwestern-border states rose to $105.5 million in 2009. But that number only reflects traditional sources of Byrne funding. The real comeback for Byrne is the massive injection of ARRA funding for criminal justice and law enforcement. In 2009 southwestern-border governors took in $432.6 million in Byrne ARRA funds for spending through 2011.

The Obama administration's decision to reverse Byrne's fortunes was no surprise to those who have followed the role of the Democratic congressional leadership in increasing federal support for state and local criminal justice operations. Nevertheless, the reversal is stunning in its proportions.

Criminal justice and drug-policy reformers consider Byrne grants and similar programs such as Community Oriented Policing Services (COPS) drug-war dinosaurs and contend that Obama's decision to pump up Byrne with stimulus funding will lead to more of the same: drug task forces that inflate statistics and increase arrests of street-level offenders in order to drive funding. Nastassia Walsh of the Justice Policy Institute told me: "We are concerned with the increased funding for police through Byrne and COPS, and especially with the ARRA, as these have [been] shown to increase arrests, especially of people of color, and increase prison populations at a time when states are looking to reduce the number of people in their prisons."

A recent Justice Policy Institute report concludes that most new Byrne funding still "goes to law enforcement, rather than prevention, drug treatment, or community services." Like the drug war abroad, the drug war at home, especially on the border, primarily targets the supply side of the drug market through enforcement and incarceration, while only marginally addressing demand issues through treatment and education. Thus Margaret Dooley-

Sammuli, Deputy State Director of the Drug Policy Alliance in San Diego, argues that every federally granted dollar spent by states on low-level arrests may generate more than $10 in new costs. The states pay for prosecution, incarceration, and other criminal justice expenses, and then deal with the consequences of recidivism when drug offenders are imprisoned without treatment.

Dooley-Sammuli, who is spearheading a campaign in California to reorient Byrne funding toward cost-saving and community-based alternatives to the incarceration of low-level nonviolent offenders, says: "This is our money, and we need to ensure that we use it to improve the criminal justice system, as the DOJ-grant guidance now advises, rather than tying it to a drug war that everyone knows has failed."

### Fear, Crime, Stray Dogs

Despite the alarm about transnational gangs, criminal enterprises, and the shocking rise in carjackings on the Mexican side, crime rates are low in large border cities. FBI crime statistics show that El Paso, where crime rates have dropped by a third over the past ten years, is the safest U.S. city with a population greater than 500,000. In 2010 there were five murders in El Paso, compared to more than 3,050 across the river in the sister city of Juárez.

The violent crime numbers in rural border counties are also reassuringly low and falling. The FBI's Unified Crime Report (UCR), which tracks major categories of crimes—murder, forcible rape, robbery, aggravated assault, burglary, larceny-theft, and arson—doesn't support the dire picture of mayhem and murder painted by border sheriffs and politicians. From 2008 to 2009 (the most recent figures publicly available for counties), the number of violent crimes fell from three to two in Sheriff West's Hudspeth County and from 46 to 39 in Gonzalez's Zapata County (population 13,792). The rate of property crimes increased in Zapata, but it's unlikely that the spike is due to drug-war violence across the border.

Since the UCR statistics challenge the sheriffs' and Perry's claims about border crime waves and spillover violence, border-area officials are seeking to reframe the debate by stressing the deterrent effect of Operations Linebacker and Border Star. "Our sheriffs are sworn to uphold the peace," explains Don Reay, Executive Director of the TBSC, "and that's what they are doing so well. It's cheaper, after all, to prevent than to arrest, prosecute, and incarcerate. Our border security operations are reducing crime on the border."

Sheriffs and officials in large border cities tend to share the federal government's assessment: drug-related violence in Mexico is not spilling over in any significant way. Sheriff Lupe Treviño of Hidalgo County, which includes the thriving border cities of Edinburg and McAllen, contends, "We haven't seen any true spillover violence on the border since 1916," when Pancho Villa and his band crossed into Columbus, New Mexico. "Certainly there are links between Mexico drug cartels and the illegal drug sales here," he tells me, "but there is no direct connection and so many degrees of separation between the Mexican cartels and U.S. drug users and street dealers that it cannot credibly be said that violence is spilling over."

"That's chamber-of-commerce talk," Gonzalez huffs, a phrase echoed by other Texas and Southwestern Coalition principals. Officials in border metropolitan areas such as El Paso, McAllen, and Brownsville downplay spillover violence and other threats to border security, he says, "out of fear that they will lose their tourists and scare away some business." Teclo Garcia, director of government relations for McAllen, disagrees. "We are, of course, not blind to the cartel violence across the border," he says, "but the image of spillover violence is promoted by politics, by those who are using violence for political gain."

El Paso County Sheriff Richard Wiles also dismisses the alarmism about spillover violence. "What we see in our community," Wiles says, "is that people are concerned with graffiti and stray dogs. All the issues of urban areas. Extreme violence is just not happening here, and we need to revisit how resources are expended on the border. That's a message to send the administration."

Still, the federal courts in Hidalgo County and other border jurisdictions are clogged with Mexican nationals. For the most part, these "criminal aliens" are not being prosecuted for the types of crimes that appear in the FBI's Uniform Crime Reporting but rather for immigration violations—illegal entry, illegal reentry, visa overstays, etc. Nationwide, more than half of the prosecutions in federal courts are for immigration violations. In the Southwest the number is far higher—more than 80 percent.

With crime comes punishment. The privately run detention centers of the U.S. Marshals Service (such as the West Texas Detention Facility in Hudspeth County), the county jails that hold the Marshals' pretrial detainees, and the privately managed criminal-alien prisons of the Bureau of Prisons in the Southwest are filling up with these criminal aliens.

## The Bandwagon Rolls On

At Neely's Crossing, my head bowed with the others, I reflect on the past and wonder about the future.

When I first came to know the border more than three decades ago, I was working with an immigrant-organizing project in Maricopa County, Arizona. I considered this strand of river, this line in the sand, mostly a point of entry and return for the Mexican *campesinos* who came to the citrus groves around Phoenix and returned to the villages in Querétaro after the picking season's end. Generally they crossed without incident, like those locals who not so long ago went back and forth at Neely's Crossing.

But times have changed, as the border sheriffs, the Border Sheriff's Posse, and political leaders such as Perry say. Violence pervades the Mexican borderlands and haunts illegal crossings. New policies are needed. Open borders are seriously considered only by the most idealistic, and the traditional acceptance of a moderate level of illegal crossing is just a memory.

I don't mind joining others in prayer, but not this one. I realize, though, that the ideological substance of Garlow's prayer is less a fringe sentiment than a fundamental reflection of the newly dominant national politics.

Before 9/11 the term used was "border control" or "border protection," and only rarely "border security" or "securing the border." But attitudes have since changed dramatically. The mission statement of Customs and Border Protection (CBP), created in 2003, dedicates the agency to protecting the homeland against "dangerous people and goods"—a clear reference in the post-9/11 environment to terrorists and weapons of mass destruction and an indication of the vastly increased scope of border operations.

The fusion of border control and national security precipitated an ongoing boom in immigration and border enforcement. As part of DHS, CBP and its brother agency, Immigration and Customs Enforcement, immediately benefited from congressional munificence. But it wasn't until 2005, as the national concern about terrorism began to diminish and the debate over immigration reform started to roil politics, that the border security bandwagon began rolling in earnest. The House Immigration Reform Caucus, then led by arch-restrictionist Tom Tancredo, launched preemptive strikes against the proposals for comprehensive immigration reform that began surfacing in Congress. Although the hard-line anti-immigrant measures mostly were defeated, they succeeded in shifting the focus of immigration reform from legalization and temporary-work programs to "enforcement-first" policy.

Moving in a parallel and sometimes intersecting path, the Bush administration in 2005 let loose its own border security zeitgeist under the leadership of DHS Secretary Michael Chertoff, who promised that year to achieve "operational control of both the northern and southern borders within five years." Bush deployed 6,000 National Guard troops to the border in mid-2006 to "deter illegal immigration." Bush accepted the restrictionists' demand that a secure border be a precondition of immigration reform. The House and Senate joined to pass the Secure Fence Act of 2006, and the Bush administration responded by making the steel fence and the proposed "virtual fence" the centerpieces of CBP's new Secure Border Initiative.

Back then border security was almost solely about immigration, but Senator Cornyn stressed at the time that the debate over immigration reform is "first and foremost about our Nation's security."

One of the early players in the merger of the immigration crackdown and border security was Congressman John Culberson, a Texas Republican and member of the House Immigration Reform Caucus. Culberson introduced the Border Law Enforcement Act of 2005, which aimed to combat the specter of "lawlessness in border areas" and brought together anti-immigration hardliners and Texas-border Democrats such as U.S. Representatives Silvestre Reyes and Henry Cuellar. The bill provided talking points that currently shape much of the border security debate and the funding process, namely that federal officials have been incapable of preventing "criminals, terrorists, and foreign nationals who have entered the United States illegally from engaging in criminal activity" and that the border's "local and state law enforcement officials are being overwhelmed by growing lawlessness." Culberson's proposal never became law, but he did come through with TBSC's $5 million earmark, the first of five it has received to date.

In 2006 the Border Law Enforcement Act largely was incorporated into the now infamous Border Protection, Anti-Terrorism, and Illegal Immigration Act of 2006, sponsored by Wisconsin Republican Jim Sensenbrenner. The bill passed the House, setting off massive pro-immigrant protests around the country. Regarded at the time as a draconian measure, some of its provisions—building a border fence, making illegal reentry a felony, involving local law enforcement in immigrant arrests—are basic elements of current border security operations.

Today the notion that lawlessness is taking over the borderlands and that the border needs securing at all costs has become a bipartisan assumption with the imprimatur of the president. Obama steadily has increased aid to border law enforcement. In August 2010 he signed a $600 million in "emergency" spending to hire patrol and customs agents and pay for communication and surveillance equipment, including unmanned aircraft. He also has deployed additional National Guard troops to the border, giving credence to the unwarranted assertions of many border politicians and law enforcement officers that the borderlands are reeling from crime.

Upgraded to a national security issue, border control is now afflicted by the fear-mongering, false threat assessments, and budget-gouging that pervade national security politics. Sheriffs, together with their federal partners, are resorting to the old drug-war and crime-fighting paradigms that have distorted domestic and foreign affairs for more than four decades. Politics and money, far more than any concerted attention on real dangerous people and goods, are driving a border security bandwagon unburdened by meaningful oversight. And with its seemingly unlimited reserves of federal dollars, the bandwagon appears unstoppable.

# 3

*Securing Arizona*

A SENSE OF SOLIDARITY LED THE TEA PARTY Patriots to Phoenix for their American Policy Summit in February 2011. It's "our opportunity to support the citizens of Arizona in their current political battles that carry so many national implications," the organizers of the Summit said. Arizona's capital, according to the Patriots, is "the great southwestern city, born from the ruins of a former civilization, now the rebirth place of American culture."

In the previous year, a few signature events—the March 2010 killing of border rancher Rob Krenz; the passage the following month of the immigration-control law SB 1070; and the January 2011 massacre in Tucson that killed six people and gravely wounded

U.S. Representative Gabrielle Giffords—focused national attention on the political and social tensions in Arizona. The state's cast of political figures—from Senator John McCain to Maricopa County Sheriff Joe Arpaio—has captured the media spotlight and won Arizona a rogue reputation.

But Arizona may not be such an outlier.

Certainly Arizona's history and geography make it one of a kind. Still, comparable demographic and cultural strife is cropping up almost everywhere in America. Arizona's budget woes, while much worse than most states', are mirrored throughout the country in conflicts over government downsizing and taxes. Hatred, economic stress, and fears of border insecurity are playing out in unusually grand scale in Arizona, yet mostly reflect a collective sense of vulnerability and uncertainty about personal and national prospects.

Arizona's politics are dominated by a potent mix of three ideological currents: support for a muscular national security program, libertarian capitalism, and social traditionalism. These ideas have long shaped the wider American conservative movement, so it is hardly surprising that some, such as the Tea Party, look to the state as a model for the nation. They applaud Arizona as the vanguard of the new conservative revolution; it has taken the challenges of immigration enforcement and border security into its own hands, opposed "big government" with its newly invigorated populism, and embraced libertarian principles through privatization and government-spending cuts. Boosters point to a mounting list of Arizona firsts: its anti-immigrant legislation, new law banning ethnic studies programs in public universities, proposals against birthright citizenship, gun-rights bills, and demand for a federal waiver from compliance with Medicaid provisions. SB 1070 copycat bills have been introduced in six states, and legislators in fifteen more have expressed interest in their own imitations.

Others see a spectacularly dangerous project in Arizona's ideological approach to policy. Instead of raising alarm about the state's financial instability,

Republican politicians—with the organized support of some prominent sheriffs, right-wing foundations and policy institutes, and the Arizona Tea Party—have exploited widespread resentment about fading wealth and diminishing social services by scapegoating immigrants and blaming Washington.

Arizona faces dire problems, but, rather than address them, its leaders make political hay out of convenient distractions. This dynamic demands close scrutiny, especially if the country is facing its future on the border.

## Bust

In the 2010 electoral season, border security talk boiled over in the Arizona heat. Governor Jan Brewer made unsubstantiated claims about drug-related beheadings; Jesse Kelly, a Tea Party candidate trying to unseat Giffords, accused her of being weak on immigration enforcement and border security; and John McCain repeatedly stressed the need to "secure our borders."

It was only on the margins that anxiety mounted over the fiscal stability of state government and the future of the badly battered Arizona economy.

You can't miss the signs of crisis. Many state parks and offices are shuttered, plastered with "Closed for Stabilization" notices. Thousands of recently built McMansions stand empty, newly constructed highway ramps lead to empty subdivisions and strip malls, and immigrants, whose cheap labor built now-abandoned housing developments, are fleeing the state as immigration enforcement intensifies.

Arizona was hit particularly hard by the housing bust thanks to its poorly diversified economy. "Five Cs"—copper, cotton, cattle, citrus, and climate—are represented on the Great Seal of Arizona, with the motto *Ditat Deus* (God Enriches). But it's been a long time since mining, ranching, and agriculture ruled Arizona. The five Cs have been reduced to one: climate. As retirees flocked to the warm sun, a "real estate–industrial complex" took root as the primary economic engine of the state.

Galloping population growth has been a constant in Arizona. Over the past four decades, the state's population has quadrupled. For the past two decades, Arizona has been the second-fastest growing state (following Nevada). Spurred by consumer demand (largely in construction and related areas), Arizona's GDP growth has far outpaced the national average.

Since the mid-1980s, easy, unsecured financing has fueled Arizona's real estate boom. As Arizonans, and later most of America, began to think of their homes as investments, waves of newcomers bought fancy new homes with the conviction that they could trade up. The boom—which outlasted the Savings and Loan scandal of the 1980s that brought heavy criticism to McCain and fellow Arizona Senator Dennis DeConcini—produced hundreds of developments stretching into the vast expanses of desert sands and paving over citrus groves that once surrounded Phoenix and other cities.

In the 1990s Arizona enjoyed enviable budget surpluses as sales and property taxes—stimulated by the housing boom—flooded government coffers. At the same time, Arizona's political leaders curried favor with voters with near-annual tax-cutting bills. As the housing bubble kept expanding and the good times kept rolling, the state legislature faithfully approved new spending packages without allocating revenues that would pay for them.

When the bubble burst in 2007, an epidemic of foreclosures and traumatic declines in housing valuations bred fiscal crisis. In 2007 Arizona was the nation's fourteenth-poorest state, but today it is second only to Mississippi. In 2009 it faced the largest income-spending gap in the nation.

No other state faces such a grave threat to its stability. A Brookings Institution study of state finances in four western states put Arizona—with its projected 33 percent budget deficit—in far worse circumstances than even California.

According to the Brookings study, in the 2011 fiscal year, Arizona faces a 12 percent cyclical budget deficit, amounting to $1.2 billion; a 21 percent structural deficit, or a cool $2.1 billion; and a loss of $2.4 billion in federal stimulus funds that propped up the state's 2010 accounts.

Instead of raising taxes, the Republican leadership has taken the fiscal crisis as an opportunity to downsize government, cut social services, and privatize. The Supreme Court building and the governor's office tower now belong to private investors, prisons are being sold off, and full-day kindergarten has been eliminated.

**Generation Gap**

Other states have suffered from the housing bust, but demographics also conspired against the stability of Arizona.

Even before the Great Recession, the state's two wellsprings of population growth—Latino immigration and Midwest migration—were proving a volatile mix. Surges of snowbirds from the north and immigrants from the south have fed Phoenix and Tucson, with brown immigrant labor building the tile-roofed homes of mostly white transplants who previously had little contact with Latinos.

The two demographic flows complemented each other economically, but the combination has proved politically toxic, especially as immigrant population growth began to outpace migration from other states. Over the last two decades, the Latino population increased 180 percent while the state shifted from 72 percent to 58 percent white. Currently, Latinos account for 31 percent of Arizona's population (yet only 17 percent of the electorate), with an estimated 7 percent of the population being unauthorized. Immigrant population growth over the past two decades has put Arizona on a fast track toward becoming a minority-majority state—likely by 2020 or sooner. It suggests rising Latino political clout and, along with it, a solid Democratic majority. Alongside Latinos, the college-educated white population has been growing faster than the senior white population and the population without college degrees, a dynamic that also disadvantages Republicans.

These changing demographics have produced a white backlash that, when combined with historically low rates of Latino electoral participation, have contributed to a Republican resurgence in Arizona.

The political backlash in part reflects a "cultural generation gap." Arizona's "swift Hispanic growth has been concentrated in young adults and children," says Brookings' William Frey, creating a population with "largely white baby boomers and older populations." In Arizona 43 percent of children are white, compared to 83 percent of seniors. The 40 percent gap is the highest in the country, far outstripping the national average of 25 percent. Other states that have experienced rapid immigrant population growth—including Nevada, California, Texas, and Florida—confront comparably wide gaps.

In addition to ethnicity and race, class shapes the state's political divide. And here again, age is a factor. With state, county, and municipal governments all strapped for cash, disparate social sectors are mobilizing to protect their own interests.

Seniors and the state's aging white population have been disproportionately affected by declining housing prices. As a result, while they don't necessarily believe that the budgets for education and indigent medical care should be slashed, they are more concerned about cuts to elderly medical care and pensions, the cost of which has jumped more than 440 percent since 2000. With everything on the chopping block, latent resentments about the disproportionate use of educational and social services by the young, poor, and Latino social sectors have emerged.

Governor Brewer describes her tax reforms as "righteous," appealing to a socially conservative, white-right base that abhors the provision of education and emergency-medical services to illegal immigrants. Never mind that, as Arizona State University economist José Mendez told *The Arizona Republic*, "Empirical studies have shown, [illegal immigrants] pay more in taxes than the value of services they receive."

Until 2007 economic growth helped to dampen the impact of these cultural and generational pressures. As long as the state could meet its public obligations, there was no reason to get anxious about immigrants ostensibly bleeding the state dry. But since then, sinking revenues from sales and property taxes have set off a frenzy of budget cutting and privatization—a frightening turn for Arizonans accustomed to boom times.

## Going Alone

Faced with this fiscal crisis, Arizona Republicans have managed to consolidate power by blaming Washington for the state's problems, exploiting fears of big government, and drawing on the state's history of anti-immigrant animus and vigilantism. Republicans occupy 61 of the 90 seats in the legislature; the governor, attorney general, secretary of state, treasurer, and superintendent of public instruction (an elected position) are all Republicans.

At the start of her new term in January 2011,

Governor Brewer set forth her "Renewed Federalism" policy agenda. "Faithful adherence to limited government and populist virtues is a hallmark of Arizona's first hundred years," Brewer declared. She vowed to pursue a model that "limits the growth of the public sector and restrains unnecessary regulatory encroachment upon areas that are outside the rightful scope of government." By "areas" she meant "the affirmative goal of stimulating free enterprise." Brewer asserted that her system "protects [Arizona] and its citizens against an over-reaching federal government," and puts the federal government's "constitutional and statutory duties to secure the border and restore integrity to our immigration system" at the top of the policy agenda.

Brewer's program hews closely to the ideology and policy prescriptions favored by the Goldwater Institute in Phoenix, Americans for Prosperity, and other conservative think tanks. The restrictionist Federation for American Immigration Reform (FAIR), for example, worked with leading Republican legislators and selected sheriffs to fashion the language of SB 1070. Both FAIR and the corporate-friendly American Legislative Exchange Council supported the formulation of SB 1070 as a model of "states' rights" immigration enforcement that other states could follow.

A key figure in charting the state's economic and social course is Republican State Senator Russell Pearce, chair of the Senate Appropriations Committee and the newly elected Senate president. Named "Taxpayer of the Year" in 2003 by the anti-tax institute Americans for Tax Reform, Pearce is a fiscal conservative, social conservative, law enforcement hardliner, and, like many key Republican leaders in Arizona, a Mormon. Pearce also closely identifies with the anti-Obama and anti–big government positions of Americans for Prosperity, which offers state-level logistical support and training to Tea Party activists. He boasts of being a "proud member" of the Tea Party.

Pearce achieved national prominence this year as the main sponsor of SB 1070 and for his outspoken views on immigrants, border security, federalism, and liberalism. A 23-year veteran of the Maricopa County Sheriff's Department, Pearce served as chief deputy under Sheriff Joe Arpaio before leaving the Department in 1994. Pearce brags that he launched the Department's notorious thousand-bed "tent city" for jailed immigrants and other selected county inmates. Since 2004 Pearce has sponsored a series of anti-immigrant measures, including bills to deny social services to unauthorized immigrants, sanction employers who hire them, make English the state's official language, prohibit ethnic-studies programs at state institutions, and deny citizenship rights in Arizona to children of illegal immigrants. Pearce is also a key figure in promoting prison privatization.

While Republican political figures such as Pearce have perfected Arizona's new conservative politics at the state level, a trio of county sheriffs—Arpaio in Maricopa County, Larry Dever in Cochise County, and Paul Babeu in Pinal County—have given critical law enforcement credibility to border security hawks who rely on popular anxiety to get elected. On the national level, Dever and Babeu have also given voice to a new border security populism, inflected more by politically effective appeals to rule of law than blatant anti-immigrant sentiment.

Dever's Cochise County is a vast swath of borderland in Arizona's southeastern corner and the heart of Representative Giffords's congressional district. Towns on either side of the 82-mile border with Mexico share the same Spanish name. In the streets of the old county seat of Tombstone, the famous gunfight at O.K. Corral between feuding gangs of deputized ruffians and rustlers is daily reenacted to crowds of fascinated tourists.

Cochise has only recently become a leading front in the border security offensive. Since the Border Patrol tightened controls along the traditional corridors of illegal crossing around El Paso and San Diego in the 1990s, flows of illegal immigrants and drugs have shifted to more inaccessible stretches of the border, such as Cochise.

Typically wearing blue jeans and a cowboy hat, Dever rejects the unholy tradition of quick-on-the-trigger Tombstone sheriffs and draws instead on moral imperative; his department's mission statement quotes Winston Churchill: "It is not enough that we do our best; sometimes we must do what is required." Interviewed at his office outside the borderland town of Bisbee, Dever insisted that local law enforcement must be involved in border control—"at least until [the] federal government decides to do its job."

Even before SB 1070 and the series of anti-immigrant legislative measures that preceded it, Cochise and Arizona were taking immigration and border issues into their own hands. One of Dever's predecessors, Sheriff Harry Wheeler, deputized a posse of Bisbee citizens, largely members of the town's anti-immigrant Loyalty League, to organize the Bisbee Deportation of 1917. The posse rounded up 1,200 suspected immigrants (both European and Mexican) for supporting the ongoing strike organized by the International Workers of the World at the Phelps

Copper mine. Wheeler loaded the suspected strikers into boxcars and, in mid-July heat, sent them 200 miles away. They were dumped without provisions or water in the middle of the New Mexico badlands.

Cochise has since proved hospitable to anti-immigrant vigilantes. Glenn Spencer, who led white-supremacist groups in California, moved in 2002 to Sierra Vista, in Cochise, where he formed the self-described citizen militia American Border Patrol "on the front lines."

Spencer befriended ranchers Roger and Don Barnett, who have a 22,000-acre ranch outside Douglas that they patrol with night-vision goggles and assault rifles. In 1999 the Barnett brothers formed a 30-member rancher militia called Cochise County Concerned Citizens. In 2009 a federal court found Roger Barnett guilty of a 2004 armed assault on a group of seven Mexican immigrants. For failing to prevent Barnett, a former county deputy, from holding unarmed Mexicans at "gunpoint, yelling obscenities at them and kicking one of the women," Dever himself was charged but not convicted in a suit organized by the Mexican American Legal Defense and Educational Fund.

Long before anti-immigrant vigilantism took an organized form in Cochise County, white ranching families on the arid cattle spreads of the borderland began lashing out against Mexican immigrants crossing their land. Only a few miles from where Krentz was murdered in 2010, the father and two brothers of a prominent ranching family of Cochise once turned their rising anger at trespassing immigrants into cruel sport.

I traveled to Cochise in 1976 after reading the preliminary news about the Hanigan brothers, Thomas and Patrick. With the support of their father George, they captured and tortured three immigrants who were passing harmlessly through their ranch on their way to seasonal farm work in northern Cochise. The young Mexican men were beaten, robbed, hanged from a tree, burnt with a flame held to their dangling feet, and threatened with knives grazing their genitals.

The Hanigans eventually cut their victims loose and told them to run back to Mexico, letting fly volleys of birdshot as they ran off. With juries sympathetic to the property owners and the alarm about drug smuggling, it took three trials for one of the Hanigans to be convicted and sentenced.

Dever and the politicians in Phoenix rely upon and cultivate this sense of go-it-alone toughness to stoke the fires of anti-immigrant sentiment and convince voters that Arizona has no choice but to come up with a homegrown response.

Phoenix Republicans also get their share of help from Sheriff Paul Babeu of Pinal County. "Sheriff Paul's" Web site urges citizens to "Stand with Arizona!" and help him "fight illegal immigration and secure the border." In frequent appearances on Fox News and any other outlet that will have him, the always-smiling, articulate, shiny-headed sheriff mixes his anti-immigrant, secure-the-border convictions with Tea Party slogans about how the country is "sprinting down the path to socialism."

With its southern edge 80 miles from the border, Pinal is not even a border county. But that doesn't bother Babeu, who is sure that violence is spilling over from Mexico into his jurisdiction and that illegal immigrants are behind a local crime wave. "With the rise in the amount of armed violent encounters in the rural areas of Pinal County, it has created a sense of fear in the general public and has restricted their ability to enjoy the desert and rural areas of the county," Babeu claimed in a recent funding proposal.

Pete Rios, chairman of the Pinal County Board of Supervisors, complains that the sheriff's department hasn't supported its threat assessment with evidence. "All I want is for the sheriff to back his claims with data, but he hasn't done that yet," Rios told me.

Rios also expressed skepticism about the sheriff's explanation of the alleged April 30, 2010 shooting of Deputy Louie Puroll by drug smugglers armed with AK-47 rifles. "They never found the AK-47s, the bales of smuggled marijuana, or even any bullet casings," Rios observed, despite helicopter surveillance and a massive dragnet that included the Border Patrol. The wounded deputy was quickly released from the hospital.

Questions about the sheriff's account of the incident and its timing—a week after Brewer signed SB 1070 to a nationwide firestorm of criticism—have since dogged the department. Forensic experts determined that Puroll's wound came from a weapon fired only inches away, fueling accusations that the shooting was a hoax to build support for SB 1070 and the sheriff himself. Babeu fired Puroll in January 2011 for tall tales he told a *Phoenix New Times* reporter about supposed contacts with drug cartels, but the sheriff stressed that he still "backed [Puroll] 100 percent" on the shootout story.

Claims by the likes of Dever and Babeu—that the federal government's failure to secure the border has subjected Arizona to spillover violence and immigrant crime—are at the core of the Arizona GOP's approach to winning elections, and Governor Brewer echoed them during the 2010 campaign. In April of that year she told of unchecked "murder, terror, and mayhem" at the border, and in June she launched the Border Security Enhancement Program, which channels money from the governor's office to border sheriffs. Announcing the program, Brewer declared, "The federal government has failed miserably in its obligation and moral responsibility to its citizens regarding border security."

Border security hawks and immigrant bashers in Arizona thrive on myths and exaggerations. Over the past decade crime rates in Arizona have dropped while the immigrant population has expanded dramatically—up 62 percent from 2000 to 2009, while Arizona's total population increased 24.6 percent. FBI crime statistics (covering all violent crime, property crime, murder, rape, robbery, assault, burglary, larceny theft, and vehicle theft) show a near-steady 22 percent decline in total crime over that period. Vehicle thefts dropped by half. Even along the border, as immigrant and non-immigrant populations were rising, crime rates fell. Douglas and Nogales, both border towns, are among the state's safest communities.

Arizona's conservative sheriffs also routinely point out that the state has become a preferred corridor for illegal immigration. In their alarm about border insecurity, they fail to note the dramatic decline in illegal crossings over the past six years. In 2010 Border Patrol apprehensions of illegal border crossers in Arizona were down by 12 percent from the previous year and were less than half the number of 2004.

**Big Government, Big Help**

The threat of escalating border violence isn't the only myth propagated by Arizona's anti-Washington activists. Border security hawks in Arizona blame the federal government for abandoning them, obligating sheriffs and the state government to cover security breaches. Brewer contributed to this narrative by establishing her Border Security Enhancement Program, but what she didn't advertise is that the

$10 million she distributed to border sheriffs (along with a subsequent $10 million to the Pinal County Sheriff's Office and other law enforcement agencies) came from the State Fiscal Stabilization Fund, established in 2009 with federal stimulus dollars from the Department of Education.

Although most of the funding was used, as intended, to stabilize the state's education budget, Brewer channeled the first $50 million in the stabilization fund to cover the payroll of the state corrections agency. While Sheriffs Dever and Babeu rail about federal neglect of the border, their departments are awash in federal dollars for border security thanks to the stimulus money and multiple large border security grants from the Departments of Homeland Security (DHS) and Justice.

Leaving the border aside, opposition to big government and the Obama administration in general plays well at the State Capitol. But conveniently missing from this narrative, too, is the back-story of federal subsidies and contracts.

At last count, Arizona received $1.19 in federal spending for every dollar sent to Washington, which makes it a beneficiary state. In contrast, California gets $0.78 back for every federal tax dollar paid, Nevada just $0.65, and Colorado $0.81, while Utah receives $1.07 and New Mexico $2.03. The taking culture of Arizona includes the state's retired masses, whose Medicare and Social Security payments not only help keep them solvent, but also direct federal government revenue to the state's still-thriving health-care sector.

Big government came to Arizona's rescue in 2009 with the American Recovery and Reinvestment Act (ARRA), which allocated $4.3 billion—nearly half of Arizona's annual budget—to stabilize the state's finances and stave off economic collapse. The termination of ARRA funding is sending shock waves through state agencies, local governments, and Arizona's education and health providers.

Arizona also benefits economically from Homeland Security contracts to house immigrant prisoners. The state already counts among its residents 2,500–3,000 immigrant detainees, and in 2009 Pinal County received $11.7 million from Immigration and Customs Enforcement to house immigrants in the 1,500-bed county jail. Increased immigration-enforcement and border security operations by the federal government in recent years have proved a boon to both private and public prisons in Arizona, and the per-diem payments offered by DHS for immigration detention will surely increase if SB 1070 is enforced.

Federal dollars also help explain Arizona's historic rise. How else to explain a housing oasis in the northern Sonoran desert? Remarking on this mystery, writer and environmental activist Edward Abbey wrote, "There is no lack of water here, unless you try to establish a city where no city should be."

Big government made this desert miracle possible with two massive water diversion projects—the Salt River Project and the Central Arizona Project (CAP). Envisioned by Barry Goldwater, CAP is the largest and most expensive aqueduct system ever constructed in the United States. Its exclusive purpose is to feed Colorado River water to parched Central and Southern Arizona. Massive pumping of groundwater, accumulated over the eons in aquifers, further enabled the desert bloom. But depleting groundwater reserves and climate change–induced drought in the Colorado Basin now loom as the most serious threats to the Arizona development model.

Direct federal subsidies also underwrite Arizona agribusiness. The United States is the third-largest producer and number-one exporter of cotton mainly because of government subsidies—more than $29 billion between 1995 and 2009, $374 million of which went to Pinal County.

## Model State, Failed State

If short-term electoral gain is the standard, Brewer's politics are good politics. But the combination of traditional anti–big government conservatism with backlash ideology may be a recipe for disaster.

For the time being, the proponents of less government and more social Darwinism—such as State Senator Pearce, the *Wall Street Journal* opinion pages, and Americans for Prosperity—aren't backing down. They insist that low taxes, immigrant crackdowns, and ridding government of the burden of social services will lead to 21st-century stability and security. Groups such as the American Legislative Exchange Council—which ranked Arizona third in the nation in its Economic Competitiveness Index in 2010—and the Tea Party Patriots continue to laud the Arizona model.

But as stimulus funds dry up and budget gaps widen, Arizonans are facing the stark consequences of their state government's anti-tax ideology and fear-mongering. Even Governor Brewer, confronting the impossible challenge of bridging the state's budget-deficit abyss, is taking sober assessment of Arizona's fundamental instability. "We face a state fiscal crisis of unparalleled dimension, one that is going to sweep over every single person in this state as well as every business and every family," Brewer warned in January 2011.

Of course, Arizona is not alone in its budget-crisis woes, which Brewer acknowledges are the worst in the state's history. Many other states and local governments also confront staggering budget deficits. Most close observers of the fiscal crises besieging state governments agree that tax increases on personal and corporate income must form part of the stabilization solution. That is the position of Arizona State University economist Tom Rex, who argues that raising taxes and fees to address the fiscal crisis in his state would have a far less negative impact than would Brewer's litany of proposed spending cuts, which, he says, will result in widespread job losses. Although tax increases inevitably carry some negative economic consequences, addressing the deficit by increasing taxes would go a long way toward staving off the kind of cyclical volatility that is roiling Arizona.

Last year the state enacted a 1 percent temporary increase in the sales tax—a sign that the Republicans' anti-tax ideology is not inflexible, but a far cry from the progressive tax reform that would help close the structural deficit. Other than that, only budget gimmicks, mandated furloughs for state employees, new debt issues, and reckless privatization schemes—along with the temporary reprieve provided by stimulus dollars—have prevented bankruptcy and government shutdown. The state treasurer is warning that issuing IOUs to state employees and debtors may be the next desperate measure.

Raising taxes is unavoidable, but so too are budget cuts. Like many other states, Arizona spends mainly in four areas: K–12 education, health care, higher education, and criminal justice and corrections. The first three have been cut dramatically, but not the fourth, which arguably creates many of the state's costliest problems. The deepening fiscal crisis could be regarded as an opportunity not only to cut criminal justice and corrections budgets but also to overhaul a penal system that incarcerates nonviolent (and overwhelmingly nonwhite) violators of drug laws.

The ideological and corporate-driven assault on government and the public goods it offers has brought Arizona's government—along with other states'—to its knees. At the same time, that assault has devastated the sense of common identity and community trust that has been the foundation of good governance in the United States.

Arizona as we now know it cannot survive, even if there is another housing boom around the corner and government budgets are stabilized. The Arizona model of sprawling, low-density desert cities was built on the myths of limitless water and perpetually cheap gas and construction labor. The entire country faces the onset of climate change and energy scarcity, but no state will confront as squarely as Arizona the consequences of its unsustainable development. Instead of moving to meet the challenges of the future, Arizona is decimating educational infrastructure; it is already demonstrating its loyalty to old ideologies over long-term planning.

There are no easy fixes, but a bit of leadership from Washington on the immigration issue might go some way toward generating a problem-solving sensibility. Arizonans, like many Americans, are right to be anxious about the federal government's largely ineffective and immensely expensive policies of border control and immigration enforcement. The surge of illegal immigration over the past two decades has in many ways enriched our economy and communities. But—occurring outside the law and in the absence of a shared national plan of sustainable economic growth—illegal immigration contributed to the erosion of our society's sense of community.

In this context Arizona's institution of SB 1070 may be understandable. But clearly its go-it-alone approach to a common problem only further divides Arizonans and the nation. The Obama administration is right to challenge the law; however, its own avid enforcement of immigration laws—resulting in record-breaking levels of prosecution, incarceration, and deportation of immigrants—is, in any honest assessment, more shameful than Arizona's as-yet unenforced immigration crackdown.

TOM BARRY    147

Immigration control is a federal responsibility, and it is the duty of the Obama administration and federal lawmakers (including the Arizona congressional delegation, led by John McCain) to outline for Americans a vision of sustainable immigration and to pass a just and enforceable immigration-reform package. Similarly, the federal government is responsible for drug policy, and its support for drug prohibition at home and drug wars abroad is a central cause of cross-border smuggling, mass incarceration, and horrific gang-related violence across Arizona's border with Mexico—as well as being a major source of the rising political influence of border security hawks.

In the wake of the Tucson massacre, border security and anti-immigration rhetoric has been toned down a notch or two. And the enormity of the budget crisis may yet create new political space in Phoenix for realistic, less ideological debate over budget priorities.

Whether Arizona can steady itself remains to be seen. But there is little reason for optimism. America's new model state may already be a failed state.

# 4

## *A New Day in the Sun Belt*

Since 9/11 a border security juggernaut has swept across the Southwest. But even as billions of dollars flow, fear and alarm about the insecurity of the border have deepened, and demands that the government do still more have grown increasingly strident. Ten years after our rush to secure our borders, it is time to change course.

Continuing the drug wars and immigration crackdowns will do nothing to increase security or safety. It will only keep border policy on the edge—teetering without direction, burdened by our failed immigration and drug policies.

Unless we address border policy in conjunction with drug policy, the drugs we consume will continue to reach us via trans-border organized crime and bloodletting in Mexico. Unless we address immigration reform, we face a future of immigrant-bashing, divided communities, stalled economies, and more immigrant prisons rising at the margins of our towns.

Concern about the federal budget deficit could bring to an end the customary large annual appropriations increases for border security and immigration enforcement, and the failures and waste accompanying those increases are becoming more apparent. We should welcome new constraints on border-security funding as an opportunity to allow reason and pragmatism to direct border policy instead of fear, politics, and money.

The standard of success for our border policy shouldn't be how completely sealed and secured our border is, but rather how well it is regulated. New regulatory frameworks for immigration and drug consumption are fundamental prerequisites for a more cost-effective border policy.

How can we achieve a new paradigm in border control? Here are eight recommendations.

## 1) Decouple Border and Immigration Control from Homeland Security

The Department of Homeland Security routinely asserts that its border-security and immigration-enforcement practices are "risk-based." Yet all evidence points to the contrary.

If we are to retain "border security" and "homeland security" as government missions, then these missions need to be more clearly defined and more narrowly focused. With new public sensitivity about deficits and economic stagnation, a comprehensive cost-benefit evaluation is in order.

The United States needs a border-security strategy that focuses on actual security threats, not on illegal drugs and illegal immigrants. In formulating such a strategy, the Department of Homeland Security should not confuse public safety with national security. Public safety is best left to law enforcement agencies and community organizations rather than being opportunistically included in an overgrown national security/homeland security apparatus.

## 2) Balance Security and Exchange

Over the past decade, the U.S. government has focused more on hindering cross-border traffic with Mexico than on facilitating the legal crossing of people and goods. Border crossings have been considered more as a threat than a fundamental benefit to both nations. Most of this attention has been focused on northbound traffic. But since 2009 the U.S. government has been increasingly monitoring—and thereby slowing—southbound traffic in order to detect flows of weapons and illegally generated cash.

U.S.-Mexico trade constitutes a palpable national interest—nearly $400 billion annually (with U.S. exports of $229 billion in 2010 much larger than $163 billion imports from Mexico). About 80 percent of this trade is carried over land.

However, the importance of binational trade and society don't imply, as many border politicians insist, that we should be spending billions of dollars more on further upgrading our ports of entry (POE) and increasing personnel.

Led by Texas Democratic Representative Silvestre Reyes and Senator John Cornyn, border politicians introduced a bill in 2010 that would provide $5 billion in emergency funding to hire 5,000 new CBP agents to staff the POEs and to upgrade the POE infrastructure. For ten years, funding has flowed from Washington for new and overhauled POEs as well as a steady expansion of CBP agents assigned to them. This was their solution to maddeningly slow border crossings that adversely affect bi-national economic relations.

Yet the main problem at the POEs is not staffing or infrastructure inadequacies. It is the intense scrutiny of all border crossers in the name of border security. In the wake of 9/11, the call for rigorous inspection practices stemmed from concerns about foreign terrorists. Over time, however, border security has come to mean more than counterterrorism— now it also means supporting Mexico's drug war. In practice the inspections are wildly disconnected from actual security threats and mostly net the products of flawed U.S. policies—such as drug prohibition and gun-rights laws that allow sales of military-grade weapons—that foster illegal cross-border flows.

The congestion at the border would greatly ease if the federal government first addressed drug reform, immigration reform, and gun control.

### 3) Don't Rush to High-Tech Solutions

Since the late 1990s the federal government has pursued an array of high-tech solutions to control the border. And when the dysfunction of the solutions—such as Integrated Surveillance Intelligence System (ISIS), which was cut off in 2004, and SBInet, which had been slowly dying since August 2008 and was cancelled in January 2011—becomes too embarrassing, the government suspends funding. Yet DHS continues to express faith in new high-tech and immensely expensive technological surveillance projects, approving contracts without any demonstration of cost effectiveness.

DHS is now considering corporate proposals for a remote, electronic surveillance system—similar to SBInet—and has yielded to demands from border politicians and industry voices for the border-wide deployment of unmanned aerial vehicles (UAVs, popularly known as "drones") without any evidence that these million-dollar systems are cost effective.

Congress should insist that DHS apply due diligence before authorizing new funding for high-tech border-security systems. There must be detailed analysis of the effectiveness of costly high-tech options. The deployment of UAVs should be terminated until the Border Patrol can demonstrate first that these unmanned aircraft reduce the need for manned aircraft and for border patrol agents and second that the UAVs, a couple of which have been deployed for several years, have proved to be a cost-effective instrument for securing the border against national security threats.

## 4) Stop New Border Spending

Politics, rather than duly considered threat assessments, have spurred border-security appropriations, but new recognition of fiscal realities may finally place limits on spending.

Cutting border funding and imposing a moratorium on new border funding won't compromise security in the name of fiscal austerity because we've never actually achieved greater security thanks to our spending. The overspending and lack of sharp focus over the past decade now create opportunities for substantial reductions in the multibillion-dollar budgets for border security without affecting security goals. Again, decisions about border-control expenditures should reflect the value of marginal gains. Until that happens, we need to stop spending.

Congress should obligate DHS, in conjunction with the Government Services Administration (which owns and maintains most POEs), to provide an evaluation of the cost and consequent security benefits of the border infrastructure and staffing buildup over the past ten years. Marginal improvements in border security should be measured against budgetary costs and adverse impact on legal cross-border trade and travel.

## 5) End Drug Prohibition and Drug Wars

After more than 40 years, it is time to bring the war on drugs to a close and end drug prohibition. Although finding the right mix of effective new drug policies—decriminalization, legalization, regulation, treatment, coerced abstinence, etc.—will depend on more study and experimentation, there is little doubt that drug prohibition and drug wars propagate criminality and violence while doing nothing to slow consumption and trafficking. Ending drug prohibition in the United States would also strike a major blow—although not a fatal one—against the spread of organized crime in Mexico and Central America.

## 6) Stop Deputizing Law Enforcement

Programs such as Operation Stonegarden, 287(g), DHS's Community Shield and Secure Communities, and the Southwest Border Initiative direct local law enforcement to border and immigration control. In the process, they divert attention away from the public-safety mission of local law enforcement agencies.

These collaborative programs, launched over the past ten years, have contributed to a serious erosion of federal authority over border control and immigration enforcement, precipitating a surge of state and local initiatives that endanger civil rights, contribute to human-rights abuses, increase budget deficits, and have little relation to public-safety concerns.

Congress should move to end Operation Stonegarden. The program, which funnels DHS funding through the Federal Emergency Management Agency (FEMA) to border law enforcement agencies, has never been subject to a performance evaluation. Stonegarden originated as a first-responder program in 2004, but now the $60–90 million it disburses annually goes mostly to border sheriffs' departments. Neither FEMA nor the Border Patrol, which approves the action plans of the border sheriffs, has monitored Operation Stonegarden. There is no accountability, no one checking for improved border control or public safety.

## 7) End Enforcement-First Immigration Policy

Enforcement-first immigration policy has been ineffective and inhumane. Predicating immigration reform on a crackdown against nation's large immigrant population in the name of the rule of law is shameful.

As a strategy for advancing immigration reform, increasing border-control operations and infrastructure is intrinsically flawed. That shouldn't be surprising given that the foundation for this strategy is the plan advanced since 2006 by immigration restrictionists. The enforcement-first strategy quickly snowballed into bipartisan calls for additional preconditions for immigration reform, including deportation of "criminal aliens," institutionalization of the "rule of law" framework for immigration policy, and "border security first." This new insistence on securing the border prior to passing immigration reform came not only from Republicans such as John McCain but also from many Democrats, including leading players in immigration reform such as New York Senator Charles Schumer.

The grand-bargain strategy has shown itself to be politically manipulative as well as an utter failure. Worse still, the strategy has recklessly bestowed a mantel of moral legitimacy on border-security buildups and immigration crackdowns.

Instead of moving the nation closer to immigration reform, the "secure the border" commitment has resulted in untold human tragedy while giving rise to ill-considered and hugely wasteful initiatives. This strategy of reform has enabled a surge in politically driven alarmism along the border.

It is time to take the grand bargain off the table and to offer a new vision of border control and immigration reform.

## 8) Concentrate on Employment

The Obama administration should—and could—end enforcement that targets immigrants who have integrated into U.S. society and workforce. The administration should make a commitment to regularize their immigration status and work with Congress to ensure immigration reform.

The new framework for immigration must also include a transparent process for issuing visas for new immigrants, and that process should be based primarily on the verified demand for their skilled and unskilled labor. This review should be safeguarded from the lobbying pressure of business interests and should ensure that new immigration will not result in job losses for current residents. ICE should focus its attention on enforcing visa expiration dates, apprehending human smugglers and traffickers, and coordinating intelligence operations with other agencies and governments.

Also essential is the enforcement of workplace safety and wage regulations, thereby precluding the now-routine exploitation of the immigrant workforce and mitigating the nationwide downward pressure on working conditions and wages.

To boost their credibility and effectiveness, liberal immigration reformers must come to the bargaining table—once the crackdown has been halted—ready to accept widespread employment verification (to dissuade new illegal-immigrant flows), stricter limits on family reunification (especially for illegal immigrants who are granted a change of immigration status), and the expansion of temporary-worker programs. Political refugees facing grave human rights abuses should be granted priority status in any assessment of the number of immigrants the nation can successfully absorb.

The stories of the Southwest—its corporate immigrant prisons, Mexican bloodbaths, wayward sheriffs, and hateful politics—illustrate the failures of our homeland security and border security policies. Other stories are possible.

To end the border wars we need different policies that address the main problems of border control:

drug flows, illegal immigration, and gun smuggling. We don't need billions of dollars in new border security funding, but rather pragmatic policy reforms, such as the ones suggested here. Sensible policy measures would diminish the pressure of illegal activity on the border, save money, and defuel the hate and fear.

With these changes, new narratives may emerge: stories of a post-drug prohibition border, shuttered prisons, a broadening consensus on immigration enforcement, Mexican communities reclaimed by civil society, and border towns recovering their cross-border heritage. Too hopeful, perhaps. But the alternative of sticking with the same border security narrative—more walls, more militarization, more invective—means opting for border wars without end.

# ACKNOWLEDGMENTS

THE SUPPORT AND ENCOURAGEMENT—AS WELL
as the excellent editing and copyediting—of the *Boston Review* editors, made *Border Wars* possible. I am
especially grateful to Deborah Chasman, the *BR* editor who invited me to submit my first article to the
magazine. It was her expert editing that turned my
draft into a cover story that helped alert the country
about the horrors of the public-private immigrant
gulag. She also encouraged me to turn other border-research projects into *BR* articles that mixed investigative reporting and public policy analysis.

What is so unusual about *BR* and what makes
it such a great magazine is the freedom it gives to
writers to explore all the interconnected policy issues of a story. In my case, *BR* gave me the room

and the support I needed to tell the story of how the associated national manias of the immigration crackdown, drug wars, private imprisonment, and border security are altering the social and political landscape of the border. Thank you, Deb, for helping me tell this story.

I also want to thank Simon Waxman, *BR*'s managing editor, for his thoughtful editing and precise copyediting. Joshua Cohen's final review of the *BR* essays included in *Border Wars* alerted me to factual and analytical shortcomings that with the help of everyone at *BR* I attempted to remedy.

At the Center for International Policy, the institute's great new deputy director, Abigail Poe, deserves my special thanks for her close review of the policy conclusions in the final chapter. Similarly, Meredith Pierce, CIP's communications specialist, helped make that a better chapter. I also want to express my appreciation to those colleagues who read parts of the manuscript and whose comments proved so helpful in clarifying the analysis and avoiding errors, including Timothy Dunn, Brady McCombs, Keoki Skinner, and Jerry Kammer.

The Nation Institute provided essential funding for the article "At War in Texas," which became the second chapter of this book. Special thanks to Esther Kaplan.

My hope is that *Border Wars* offers a grounded and insightful view of the escalation of the border security wars in the Southwest. In my travels along the borderlands—from the deserts and mountains of Arizona and Sonora, through West and South Texas, and to the mouth of the Rio Grande as it enters the Gulf of Mexico—many activists, reporters, and officials helped me follow the story, and they too helped make this book. Yet any factual errors or analytical lapses that may have slipped in are entirely my responsibility.

# ABOUT THE AUTHOR

TOM BARRY is Director of the TransBorder Project at the Center for International Policy. He has authored and coauthored more than twenty books, including *The Great Divide: The Challenge of U.S.-Mexico Relations in the 1990s* and *Zapata's Revenge: Free Trade and the Farm Crisis in Mexico*. A version of "A Death in Texas," which first appeared in the November/December 2009 issue of *Boston Review*, was a finalist for the National Magazine Award in the Public Interest category.

Tom blogs at borderlinesblog.blogspot.com and lives in a small town in the mountains of southwestern New Mexico.

# BOSTON REVIEW BOOKS

Boston Review Books is an imprint of *Boston Review*, a bimonthly magazine of ideas. The book series, like the magazine, is animated by hope, committed to equality, and convinced that the imagination eludes political categories. Visit bostonreview.net for more information.